A QUICK REVIEW OF GLOBAL HISTORY

Second Edition

Everything You Need to Know to Pass the Regents Examination

JAMES KILLORAN
STUART ZIMMER
MARK JARRETT

JARRETT PUBLISHING COMPANY

East Coast Office:
P. O. Box 1460
Ronkonkoma, NY 11779
631-981-4248

West Coast Office:
10 Folin Lane
Lafayette, CA 94549
925-906-9742

1-800-859-7679   Fax 631-588-4722

www.jarrettpub.com

ABOUT OUR COVER

The Taj Mahal in the city of Agra in India is one of the most famous buildings in the world. Built during the reign of Shah Jahan (1628-1658) as a tomb for his beloved wife, it is said to have taken 20,000 workers more than 15 years to construct. It is built of white marble on a red sandstone base and is surrounded by magnificent gardens.

Jarrett Publishing Company
P. O. Box 1460
Ronkonkoma, New York 11779

ISBN 1-882422-46-5

Copyright 2006 Jarrett Publishing Company
Printed in the United States of America by
Malloy, Inc., Ann Arbor, Michigan
Second Edition
10 9 8 7 6 5 4   10 09 08

ACKNOWLEDGEMENTS

The authors would like to thank Kevin Sheehan, Oceanside High School, Oceanside, New York, for his comments, suggestions and recommendations.

Layout and typesetting by Maple Hill Press, Huntington NY.

This book is dedicated

...to my wife Donna, my children Christian, Carrie and Jesse, and
my grandson Aiden — *James Killoran*

...to my wife Joan, my children Todd and Ronald, and my
grandchildren Jared and Katie — *Stuart Zimmer*

...to my wife Goska and my children Alexander and Julia — *Mark Jarrett*

ABOUT THE AUTHORS

James Killoran, a retired Assistant Principal, has written many social studies books. He has extensive experience in test writing for the N.Y. State Board of Regents in social studies and has served on the Committee for Testing of the National Council of Social Studies. His article on social studies testing has been published in *Social Education*, the country's leading social studies journal. Mr. Killoran has won many awards for outstanding teaching and curriculum development, including "Outstanding Social Studies Teacher" and "Outstanding Social Studies Supervisor" in New York City. In 1993, he was awarded an Advanced Certificate for Teachers of Social Studies by the N.C.S.S. In 1997, he served as Chairman of the N.C.S.S. Committee on Awarding Advanced Certificates for Teachers of Social Studies.

Stuart Zimmer, a retired social studies teacher, has written numerous social studies books. He served as a test writer for the N.Y. State Board of Regents in Social Studies, and has written for the National Merit Scholarship Examination. He has published numerous articles on teaching and testing in social studies journals. He has presented many demonstrations and educational workshops at state and national teachers' conferences. In 1989, Mr. Zimmer's achievements were recognized by the New York State Legislature with a Special Legislative Resolution in his honor.

Mark Jarrett, a former social studies teacher, has written many social studies books. Mr. Jarrett has served as a test writer for the N.Y. State Board of Regents, and has taught at Hofstra University. He was educated at Columbia University, the London School of Economics, the Law School of the University of California at Berkeley, and Stanford University. Mr. Jarrett has received several academic awards including the Order of the Coif at Berkeley and the David and Christina Phelps Harris Fellowship at Stanford. He worked as an attorney for ten years with the international law firm of Baker & McKenzie.

TABLE OF CONTENTS

SKIPPING THE FIRST THREE CHAPTERS COULD BE HAZARDOUS TO YOUR SUCCESS!

CHAPTER 1

THE BASIC TOOLS OF GLOBAL HISTORY

OVERVIEW

This book is designed to provide you with a quick review of the material you will need to know for the Global History and Geography Regents Examination. This chapter provides techniques to help you remember important information. Chapter 2 will help you answer thematic essay questions. Chapter 3 focuses on how to answer document-based essay questions.

The later chapters of the book provide nine content reviews that summarize the main developments in global history. Each of these chapters opens with a section that identifies the major themes of the particular era. It is followed by a short summary of the historical developments of that period in global history. Each content chapter closes with a series of questions that test your understanding of the era.

Following the content reviews, you will find a final review that includes:

- the most important concepts and terms of global history
- organizers on major themes for you to complete
- regional study guides organized chronologically

The book concludes with a full-length practice Global History and Geography Regents Examination.

REMEMBERING INFORMATION

Examination questions often test your knowledge of important terms, concepts, and people in global history and geography. This section discusses ways to make it easier for you to remember important information so that you can improve your performance on the Global History and Geography Regents Examination.

1

TERMS

Terms refer to specific things that actually happened or existed, such as particular places or events. Questions about a term usually ask about its main features:

what it is (or was)   *its purpose*   *its causes and effects*   *its significance*

CONCEPTS

Concepts are words or phrases that refer to categories of information. They allow us to organize large amounts of information. For example, Italy, Nigeria, and China share common characteristics. The concept *country* acts as an umbrella, grouping these specific "examples" by identifying what they have in common. Questions about concepts usually ask for a definition or an example of the concept. Thus, when you study a concept, you should learn the following:

its significance

an example

FAMOUS PEOPLE

In global history you will also learn about many famous people. Test questions about these individuals will usually ask you who they are and why they are famous. Therefore, when you study a famous person, it is important to learn:

the place and time period in which the person lived   *his or her background or position*   *the person's accomplishment or impact*

To help you remember important terms, concepts, and people, you should complete an index card for each one.

❖ **Front of Card**: Write out the important information.

❖ **Back of Card**: Draw a picture about the information on the front.

Look at the following example for the term Magna Carta:

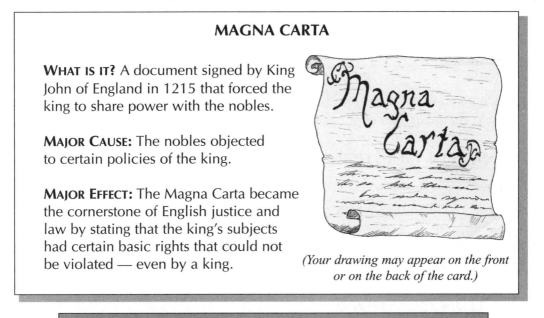

MAGNA CARTA

WHAT IS IT? A document signed by King John of England in 1215 that forced the king to share power with the nobles.

MAJOR CAUSE: The nobles objected to certain policies of the king.

MAJOR EFFECT: The Magna Carta became the cornerstone of English justice and law by stating that the king's subjects had certain basic rights that could not be violated — even by a king.

(Your drawing may appear on the front or on the back of the card.)

ANSWERING DATA-BASED QUESTIONS

Knowing how to interpret different types of data is crucial to performing well on multiple-choice and document-based essay questions. Some questions will present their own data in the question. The types of data most often found on these questions are:

- Maps
- Line Graphs
- Tables
- Political Cartoons
- Speaker Questions
- Bar Graphs
- Pie Charts
- Timelines
- Outlines
- Reading Passages

Almost all data-based questions can be grouped into four general types: comprehension, conclusion, explanation, and prediction.

COMPREHENSION QUESTIONS

These questions ask you to find a specific item, figure, or number presented in the data. A comprehension question may take any of the following forms:

❖ According to the chart, in which year was production the greatest?
❖ In 1800, the greatest population growth occurred in which country?

CONCLUSION OR GENERALIZATION QUESTIONS

These questions ask you to draw a *conclusion* or make a *generalization* by tying together several elements found in the data presented. These questions may take any of the following forms:

❖ Which generalization is most accurate, based on the data?
❖ What is the main idea of the data?

EXPLANATION QUESTIONS

These questions ask you to provide an *explanation* for the situation illustrated by the data. Such questions may take any of the following forms:

❖ The problem illustrated in the cartoon was caused by ...
❖ Which factor contributed most to the change shown on the graph?

PREDICTION QUESTIONS

These questions ask you to make a *prediction* based on the situation illustrated in the data. Such questions may take one of the following forms:

❖ Which may be a result of the situation shown in the data?
❖ Based on the information in the data, which is most likely to occur?

DEVELOPING A SENSE OF TIME AND PLACE

It is very important to have a good grasp of **time** and **place** when studying global history and geography. The range of global history covers a vast period of time — from the beginning of humankind to the present — and touches all areas of the world. In order to understand this vast sweep, you must do the following:

• First, you must have a strong general sense of the basic time periods of global history, including the major beliefs, ideas, technologies, and events of each period.

• Second, you must know the main geographical features of the world — the stage on which these historical developments unfolded.

DEVELOPING A SENSE OF TIME

Historians often divide history into time periods (*eras*) — spans of time unified by common characteristics. There is no exact agreement on historical periods and their dates. Traditionally, historical periods have been tied to a particular region or culture. For example, the Middle Ages is a historical period closely tied to Europe, while the Ming Dynasty refers to a period in the history of China. More recently, historians have attempted to identify major eras that affected all regions. This book divides the history of the world into eight such eras, each with its own unique features:

ERAS OF WORLD HISTORY

1. The Dawn of Civilization, 3500 B.C. to 500 B.C.
2. The Classical Civilizations, 500 B.C. to 500 A.D.
3. New Centers of Culture in an Age of Turmoil, 500 A.D. to 1200 A.D.
4. Warriors on Horseback and the Revival of Europe, 1200 to 1500
5. The Birth of the Modern World, 1450 to 1770
6. New Currents: Revolution, Industry and Nationalism, 1770 to 1914
7. The World at War, 1914 to 1945
8. From Cold War to Global Interdependence, 1945 to the present

Based on your previous study of global history, you should be able to identify some of the major characteristics of each era.

DEVELOPING A SENSE OF PLACE

Now, let's look at the regions of the world and their major geographical characteristics.

AREA	COUNTRIES	MAJOR GEOGRAPHIC FEATURES
North America	Canada, United States, Mexico, Caribbean Islands	• Its location, bordered by the Atlantic and Pacific Oceans, isolated it from Africa, Asia, and Europe until the 1500s. • Its mountain ranges mainly extend along its western side from Canada into Mexico
South America	Argentina, Bolivia Brazil, Colombia, Chile, Ecuador, Paraguay, Peru, Uruguay, Venezuela	• Its location near the equator makes much of the region's climate warm • The Amazon rain forest *(the world's largest)*, occupies most of northeastern South America • The Andes Mountains run along the western side of South America

continued...

AREA	COUNTRIES	MAJOR GEOGRAPHIC FEATURES
Europe	Austria, British Isles, France, Germany, Greece, Italy, Portugal, Spain, others	• The Pyrenees Mountains and the Alps separated European peoples; they developed different languages and cultures • The Rhine, Danube, and other rivers allowed Europeans to trade with each other easily • Much of northern Europe is a plain with few defensible borders
Middle East/ North Africa	Algeria, Egypt, Iran, Iraq, Israel, Jordan, Libya, Morocco, Tunisia	• Much of the region is desert; it lacks plentiful water • Most of the people live along rivers or coasts where there is enough water to grow crops • The region provides about half the world's oil supply
Sub-Saharan Africa	Angola, Congo, Ghana, Kenya, Nigeria, South Africa, Tanzania, Zaire, Zimbabwe, others	• This region is south of the Sahara Desert • Much of the region is savanna, good land for crops and livestock • Central and Southwest Africa are mainly tropical rain forests • Mountains, deserts, and few navigable rivers separated peoples; they developed many different cultures and languages
Northern Asia	Northern Russia, Mongolia	• Northernmost Russia is tundra, with the ground frozen much of the year • Siberia, in western Russia, has valuable timber, oil, gas, and minerals • Because of Russia's great distance from Western Europe, its culture developed independently
Central Asia	Southeast Russia, Western China, Kazakhstan, Uzbekistan, others	• Central Asia was once a crossroads for overland trade routes between China, India, the Middle East, and Europe. • The steppes of the region provide excellent grazing land, and allowed its people to become herders and to excel at horsemanship; Central Asian warriors often invaded other areas
East Asia	China, Japan, Korea	• China's southern and western borders are ringed by mountains, which isolated it from the outside world • Japan is small, with 85% of its land covered by mountains • Japan lacks natural resources necessary for modern industry, such as coal and oil • Japan's high population density has promoted social cooperation
South Asia	Bangladesh, India, Pakistan	• The Himalayas, the world's highest mountains, separate the Indian subcontinent from the rest of Asia • Along the Ganges, Indus, and Brahmaputra Rivers are fertile plains with very high population densities • Monsoons bring heavy summer rains for growing crops, but sometimes cause destructive flooding
Southeast Asia	Cambodia, Laos, Indonesia, Malaysia, Philippines, Thailand, Vietnam	• The region is surrounded by the Pacific and Indian Oceans • The shortest water route between the Pacific and Indian Oceans runs through this region • The region is the "rice bowl" of Asia, and is heavily affected by the monsoon season • Islands of Southeast Asia that grew prized spices such as pepper and cinnamon were fought over by Europe's colonial powers

CHAPTER 2

HOW TO ANSWER
THEMATIC ESSAY QUESTIONS

An essay question measures your ability to present information in written form. The Global History and Geography Regents Examination will include one thematic essay.

THEMATIC ESSAY QUESTIONS

A thematic essay question requires you to focus on a particular theme or generalization. Let's look at a typical thematic essay question:

Directions: Write a well-organized essay that includes an introduction, several paragraphs explaining your position, and a conclusion.

Theme: **Geography**

> The geographical features of an area often affect historical developments taking place there.

Task:

Choose *two* past civilizations from your study of global history and geography.

For *each* civilization:
- Describe a geographical feature that affected it.
- Explain how that feature had an impact on that civilization. You may use a different feature for each civilization.

You may use any example from your study of global history and geography. Some suggestions you might wish to consider are: Egypt, the ancient Greeks, the Byzantine Empire, and the Mongol Empire. **You are *not* limited to these suggestions.**

Notice that a thematic essay question opens with a general statement that identifies a common pattern. This type of statement, known as a *generalization*, shows what several facts have in common. Here, the generalization is about the impact of geography.

The question then gives you a task to complete. The directions tell you the form in which the essay must be written. The suggestions provide helpful examples you might use to support the opening statement. Thus, you are asked:

❖ to show your understanding of a generalization by using specific examples that support it, and

❖ to write a well-organized essay that includes an introduction, several paragraphs explaining your position, and a conclusion.

THE "ACTION WORDS" OF ESSAY QUESTIONS

Essay questions require you to understand certain key words. The exact instructions for what you are supposed to do in writing your answer are contained in the "action words." The most common "action words" are:

Describe
or
Discuss

Explain
or
Show How

Explain
or
Show Why

In this section, we will examine each of these "action words" to see specifically what they require you to do when answering an essay question.

DESCRIBE/DISCUSS

Describe or **discuss** means to "tell about something in words." Describe or discuss questions ask for the **"who," "what," "when,"** and **"where"** of something. Not every describe or discuss question requires all four of these elements, but you must write several paragraphs. The following are examples of *describe* and *discuss* questions:

✦ *Describe* a scientific achievement that occurred during the Renaissance.
✦ *Discuss* two changes brought about by the French Revolution.

Note how the first question asks you to *describe* a particular scientific achievement. Your answer should create a verbal picture of **who** (*Nicholas Copernicus*), **what** (*his conclusion that the sun was at the center of the solar system*), **when** (*Renaissance era*), and **where** (*Europe*). **Hint**: go through a mental checklist of *who, what, when,* and *where,* whenever you are asked to *describe* or *discuss* something.

EXPLAIN AND SHOW

Explain and **show** are often linked with the additional word *how* or *why*. The key in approaching any question with these action words is to determine whether the question requires you to give an answer for *how* something happened or *why* it happened.

❖ **HOW QUESTIONS.** These questions ask you to explain how something works or how it relates to something else. Let's look at two examples:

- *Show how* feudalism created a new system of government in Western Europe during the Middle Ages.
- *Explain how* new technology often affects a country's economic development.

> Notice how the first question asks you to give facts and examples to show the way in which the statement is true. Such facts might include (1) *when* feudalism developed; (2) *why* it came about; (3) *how* it worked; and (4) *how* it provided a new system of government. Be sure that the parts of your answer (*facts and examples*) "support" the general statement, and that the general statement answers the question.

❖ **WHY QUESTIONS.** *Explain why* or *show why* questions focus on causes (*the reasons why*). Your answer should identify the reason why an event or relationship took place and briefly describe each reason. Two examples of such questions are:

- *Explain why* the first civilizations emerged six thousands years ago.
- *Show why* feudalism developed in Japan.

> Notice how the first question asks you to *explain* the reasons *why* the first civilizations emerged. You should go through a mental checklist of various reasons or causes to be sure they add up to a satisfactory explanation.

WRITING A WELL-ORGANIZED ESSAY

Let's practice writing a thematic essay by answering the model question on page 7.

❖ Start by looking at the Task. Be sure you understand what it asks you to do.
❖ Focus on what <u>you need</u> to do by <u>underlining</u> the "action words."
❖ Circle the *number of examples* the question requires.

NOTES FOR YOUR ESSAY

Taking notes before writing is important in helping you to organize your essay. Use this sample as your guide for taking notes:

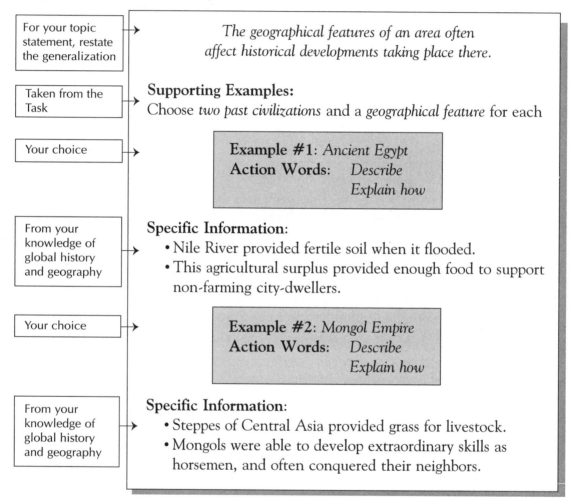

For your topic statement, restate the generalization →

The geographical features of an area often affect historical developments taking place there.

Taken from the Task →

Supporting Examples:
Choose *two past civilizations* and a *geographical feature* for each

Your choice →

Example #1: *Ancient Egypt*
Action Words: *Describe*
                          Explain how

From your knowledge of global history and geography →

Specific Information:
• Nile River provided fertile soil when it flooded.
• This agricultural surplus provided enough food to support non-farming city-dwellers.

Your choice →

Example #2: *Mongol Empire*
Action Words: *Describe*
                          Explain how

From your knowledge of global history and geography →

Specific Information:
• Steppes of Central Asia provided grass for livestock.
• Mongols were able to develop extraordinary skills as horsemen, and often conquered their neighbors.

USING THE "CHEESEBURGER" METHOD

Now let's use the information from your notes to write a thematic essay. Imagine your answer resembles a cheeseburger, with a top bun, a slice of cheese, patties of meat, and bottom bun. The top bun is your **topic sentence**. The cheese slice is your **transition sentence**. These two parts make up your first paragraph. The patties of meat are the **body of your essay** with your supporting statements. The bottom bun is your **conclusion**. In writing your essay, be sure to include all these parts.

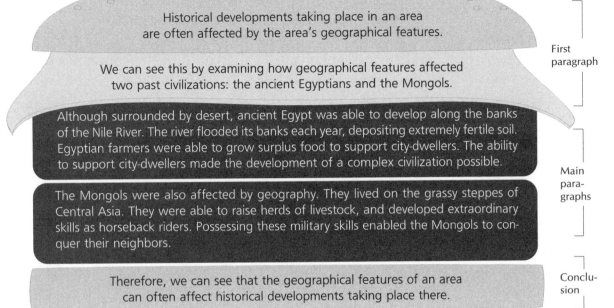

Historical developments taking place in an area are often affected by the area's geographical features.

First paragraph

We can see this by examining how geographical features affected two past civilizations: the ancient Egyptians and the Mongols.

Although surrounded by desert, ancient Egypt was able to develop along the banks of the Nile River. The river flooded its banks each year, depositing extremely fertile soil. Egyptian farmers were able to grow surplus food to support city-dwellers. The ability to support city-dwellers made the development of a complex civilization possible.

Main para-graphs

The Mongols were also affected by geography. They lived on the grassy steppes of Central Asia. They were able to raise herds of livestock, and developed extraordinary skills as horseback riders. Possessing these military skills enabled the Mongols to conquer their neighbors.

Therefore, we can see that the geographical features of an area can often affect historical developments taking place there.

Conclusion

TOP BUN *(TOPIC SENTENCE)*

Your first sentence should provide the topic of the essay. This sentence states the main idea, or thesis, of the essay so that your reader knows exactly what your position is. To write the topic or thesis sentence, often you can take the generalization from the Theme part of the question (see page 7) and express it in a different form, as we have done here on the top bun of the "cheeseburger."

These make up your first paragraph

CHEESE SLICE *(TRANSITION SENTENCE)*

The "cheese" sentence connects the topic statement to the more specific information you are about to give. This sentence introduces the next section and also helps the reader follow your thoughts by connecting your topic statement with the main part of the essay.

PATTIES OF MEAT *(MAIN PARAGRAPHS)*

Here you give specific examples and facts to support your topic statement. This is the main part of your essay. Notice how the two main paragraphs in the "cheeseburger" correspond to the examples in your notes on page 10.

BOTTOM BUN (CONCLUSION)

The last part of your essay should be similar to your first sentence (the topic sentence), except that it is now expressed as a conclusion. There are several ways to state your conclusion:

Therefore, we can see that ...   — or —   *Thus, it is clear that ...*

Notice how the closing sentence reminds the reader of the topic statement and informs the reader that the essay has come to an end.

THEMATIC ESSAY TOPICS

Thematic essays on the New York State Regents Examination will test your knowledge of the following fifteen themes:

- Belief Systems
- Change
- Culture/Intellectual Life
- Diversity
- Economic Systems
- Environment
- Geography
- Imperialism
- Interdependence
- Justice and Human Rights
- Movement of People and Goods
- Nationalism
- Political Systems
- Science and Technology
- Urbanization

The following chart summarizes some of the types of thematic essay questions on the test:

THEME	COMMON THEMATIC ESSAY QUESTIONS
Geography	Questions on the impact of geography: • **Middle East**: abundance of oil, shortage of water • **Europe**: flat plains left nations open to invasion • **Africa**: Vast natural resources prompted European imperialism • **Southeast Asia**: Monsoon rains bring needed water but also destructive floods • **South America**: Mountains and rain forests isolated groups, leading to a variety of cultures
Political Systems	Questions on major political systems: • Democracy • Absolutism • Feudalism • Fascism • Divine Right • Totalitarianism

Continued ...

THEME	COMMON THEMATIC ESSAY QUESTIONS
People	Questions on people from a wide variety of cultures: • **China**: Kublai Khan, Mao Zedong, Sun Yat-Sen, Deng Xiaoping • **Russia**: Peter the Great, Catherine the Great, Lenin, Stalin, Gorbachev, Yeltsin • **Africa**: Mansa Musa, Kwame Nkrumah, Nelson Mandela • **Europe**: Alexander the Great, Charlemagne, Napoleon, Adolf Hitler • **Middle East**: Anwar Sadat, Menachem Begin, Ayatollah Khomeini, Saddam Hussein • **India**: Asoka the Great, Akbar the Great, Mohandas Gandhi • **Latin America**: Simon Bolivar, Fidel Castro
Belief Systems	Questions on the founders, beliefs and major practices of world religions: • **Judaism**: Moses • **Christianity**: Jesus • **Islam**: Mohammed • **Buddhism**: Siddhartha Gautama • **Hinduism**: Reincarnation • **Confucianism**: Confucius
Change	Questions on major events around the world: • **Europe**: Fall of Rome, Fall of Constantinople, Protestant Reformation • **India**: Sepoy Mutiny • **Japan**: Perry's Arrival, Meiji Restoration, Atomic Bomb dropped • **China**: Boxer Rebellion, Tiananmen Square Uprising • **Southeast Asia**: Vietnam War • **Middle East**: Birth of Islam, Intifada • **Russia**: Dissolution of the Soviet Union • **Latin America**: Encounter with Europeans
Revolutions	Questions on the causes and effects of major revolutions: • Neolithic Revolution • Russian Revolution • Scientific Revolution • Chinese Revolution • French Revolution • Cuban Revolution • Industrial Revolution • Iranian Revolution
Wars	Questions on the causes and effects of major wars: • Crusades • Hindu-Muslim Wars • Wars of Religion • Cold War • World War I • Vietnam War • World War II • Arab-Israeli Wars
Science and Technology	Questions on the impact of science and technology on society: • Electricity • Medical transplants • Automobile • Space exploration • Atomic bomb • Computers • Antibiotics • Internet

CHAPTER 3

HOW TO ANSWER DOCUMENT-BASED ESSAY QUESTIONS

The Global History and Geography Regents will require you to answer one **document-based essay question,** sometimes referred to as a "D.B.Q." This type of question tests your ability to interpret historical documents and data. Let's begin by looking at a simplified document-based essay question, dealing with the French Revolution.

A SAMPLE QUESTION

This task is based on the accompanying documents 1-3. Some of these documents have been edited for the purposes of this task. This task is designed to test your ability to work with historical documents. As you analyze the documents, take into account both the source of the document and the author's point of view.

Directions: Read the documents in Part A and answer the questions after each document. Then read the directions for Part B and write your essay.

Historical Context:
During the late 1700s, a revolution occurred in France which greatly affected not only France but the rest of the world.

Task:
Discuss the political and social changes brought about by the French Revolution.

Turn to Part A

Part A
Short Answer

Directions: Analyze the documents and answer the questions that follow each document in the space provided.

Note: On most D.B.Q.s there are 5-8 pieces of data. At least two will be documents other than reading passages, such as cartoons or pictures. To simplify our explanation, this sample question has only three documents.

DOCUMENT 1

"1. Men are born and remain free and equal in rights; social distinctions can be established only for the common benefit.

2. The aim of every political association is the conservation of the natural rights of man; these rights are liberty, property, security, and resistance to oppression.

3. The source of all sovereignty is located in essence in the nation; no body, no individual, can exercise authority which does not emanate from it expressly."

Declaration of the Rights of Man and of the Citizen
August 20-26, 1789

1. According to the document, what is the purpose of every government? _____

_____

DOCUMENT 2

"The National Assembly decrees that hereditary nobility is forever abolished; in consequence, the titles of prince, duke, count, marquis, viscount, baron, knight ... and all other similar titles, shall neither be taken by anyone nor given to anyone."

Decree of the National Assembly
June 19, 1790

2. What would be the effect of this decree on the nobility of France? _____

_____

DOCUMENT 3

3. What was the significance of the king's execution?

_____

_____

The beheading of Louis XVI

Part B — Essay

Directions:
- Write a well-organized essay that includes an introduction, several paragraphs, and a conclusion.
- Use evidence from the documents to support your response.
- Do not simply repeat the contents of the documents.
- Include specific related information.

Task: Using information from the documents and your knowledge of global history and geography, write an essay in which you:

Discuss the political and social changes brought about by the French Revolution.

USING THE L•A•W APPROACH

Notice that document-based essay questions have the following parts:
  (1) directions on what to do;
  (2) a historical generalization that sets the stage for the essay question;
  (3) a task you must perform, stated in the form of a question;
  (4) Part A, with up to 8 documents that must be analyzed; and
  (5) Part B, with directions for writing your essay.

You need to focus on three areas: (1) look at the task; (2) analyze the documents; and (3) write the essay. To remember this three-pronged approach, think of the word "L•A•W."

"L" — LOOK AT THE TASK

First look at the "Task" part of the question on page 14. Focus on (1) the "**action word**," in this case *discuss*, and (2) the **topic statement**—that political and social changes were caused by the French Revolution. These determine how you will answer the question.

"A" — ANALYZE THE DOCUMENTS

As you read each document, think about (1) who wrote it; (2) the time period when it was written; (3) the purpose for which it was written; and (4) what it says. Then answer the question that follows each document. These questions help you pinpoint important information for your essay, and will be scored as part of your essay.

An **Analysis Box** can help you to analyze the documents and link them to your essay. Be sure you show *how information in the documents supports your topic statement.* You can include other related information at the bottom of the box.

Document	Main Idea	Political	Social
Rights of Man	*This excerpt states that people are born free with equal rights, and that the purpose of government is to protect these rights. It also states that the source of political power is the nation (the people).*	✓	✓
National Assembly Decree	*This decree abolished hereditary nobility in France.*		✓
Execution of Louis XVI	*In 1793, Louis XVI was beheaded. There was no turning back now. Republican spirit spread throughout France.*	✓	✓
Additional related information:			
• *During the Revolution, chaos and violence erupted throughout France.*		✓	
• *In the "Reign of Terror," many nobles and priests were beheaded by revolutionaries.*			✓
• *Revolutionary France became involved in a war against the monarchies of Europe.*		✓	
• *All French people called each other "citizen," and aristocratic fashions were replaced by simpler clothes.*			✓

Let's look at the information in the Analysis Box:

❖ In the **Document** column, you should write a brief term or phrase to identify each document. For example, since the first document was a quotation from the *Declaration of the Rights of Man*, you might simply write "Rights of Man" in the first box.

❖ In the **Main Idea** column, briefly describe the main idea of each document. Remember that the answer to the question accompanying each document will often guide you to the most important information.

❖ The final column depends on what you have to cover in your essay. Here, in the *Political* and *Social* columns, a check (✔) is put in the column if the information in the document deals with that topic. For example, since the first document deals with political aspects of the French Revolution, a check is placed in the political column.

❖ The directions ask you to include **additional information** about the topic, based on your knowledge of global history. Here, for example, you might add information about the "Reign of Terror."

"W" — WRITE THE ESSAY

In writing your essay answer, the key points to remember are:

❖ **Opening Paragraph.** The opening sentence should identify the topic and set the time and place for the reader. The next sentence should identify the main idea of your essay. Remember, you can take this from the statement found in the directions that appear in "Part B — Essay." Next, write a transition sentence to lead the reader to the supporting paragraphs.

❖ **Supporting Paragraphs.** These paragraphs provide evidence to support the topic statement. They must include references to the documents as well as additional related information from your knowledge of global history.

❖ **Conclusion.** How you close the essay depends on the action word used in the question:

• If the question asks you to **discuss**, your conclusion should restate the topic statement. For example, "We can see that the French Revolution brought about many political and social changes." You might add a brief summary from the body of your essay showing that it is an accurate thesis, such as: "Doing away with the monarchy and the nobility demonstrated the extent of these changes."

• If the question asks you to **evaluate**, your conclusion should compare and contrast the positive and negative effects, and then make a judgment. For example, if you were asked to "evaluate" the political and social impact of the French Revolution, you might compare the advantages of abolishing the monarchy, nobility, and feudalism with the disadvantages of war and violence. Then sum up: "On balance, the Revolution was worth the costs. It created a society based on merit, not inherited privilege."

CHAPTER 4

THE RISE OF CIVILIZATION, 3500 B.C. to 500 B.C.

The first human beings appeared in East Africa between 200,000 and 400,000 years ago. Gradually, humans spread around the world. Some groups developed farming and built permanent settlements. Eventually, settlements in the river valleys of Africa and Asia developed into the world's first civilizations. The study of ancient civilizations helps us to understand the basic problems all societies face — how to organize to meet human needs. By studying past civilizations, we also develop a greater awareness of the tremendous debt we owe to those who came before us.

Library of Congress

Iron tools have been used in Africa since ancient times

OUR DEBT TO THE WORLD'S FIRST CIVILIZATIONS

- **Writing.** The ancient invention of writing allowed vast amounts of human knowledge to be recorded and passed down from one generation to the next.

- **Food and Clothing.** Even today, many of our foods and clothing styles reflect the legacy of ancient cultures.

- **Forms of Expression.** Much of modern language, literature, and art closely follows what was done in ancient times.

- **Math and Science.** Our knowledge of science and mathematics is built on the foundations of ancient discoveries and inventions.

In studying this era, you should focus on the following questions:

- ✦ What were the consequences of the Neolithic Revolution?
- ✦ What factors led to the rise of the first civilizations?
- ✦ What were the most important contributions of early civilizations?

THE FIRST HUMAN BEINGS

Early human beings passed on their culture to their children. **Culture** refers to a people's way of life, including their language, clothes, shelter, tools, family organization, beliefs, system of government, and ways of obtaining food.

Early humans relied on hunting, fishing, and gathering wild plants for food. The search for food led people to migrate from Africa to other parts of the world. About 10,000 years ago, people in the Middle East discovered how to plant the seeds of grain to grow their own food. They also learned to raise animals such as sheep, goats, and cattle. These advances, referred to as the **Neolithic Revolution**, allowed people to build permanent homes and villages and adopt a settled way of life.

RISE OF RIVER VALLEY CIVILIZATIONS

A **civilization** is an advanced form of human culture in which some of the people of a society live in cities, have a form of writing, and are skilled at science and technology. About 3500 B.C., the world's first civilizations emerged in river valleys. Rivers in these regions tended to overflow each year, depositing fertile soil along their banks. This allowed people in the area to grow large food surpluses to support an urban (*city*) population. There were four important river valley civilizations in ancient times:

MESOPOTAMIA (3500 B.C. - 1700 B.C.)

Ancient Mesopotamia was the region between the Tigris and Euphrates Rivers, in present-day Iraq. The Sumerians, one of the first peoples in this area, invented the wheel and the sailboat, created a twelve month calendar, developed cuneiform symbol-writing on clay tablets, and made the first objects of copper and bronze. Babylonians later conquered this region and developed the world's first law code — the **Code of Hammurabi**. Some of the code's provisions punished criminals quite harshly, stressing the idea of "an eye for an eye, and a tooth for a tooth." The area was later conquered by the Hittites, Assyrians, Chaldeans, and Persians.

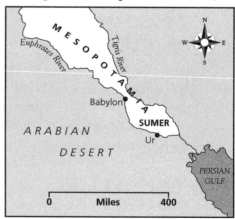

EGYPT (3200 B.C.- 500 B.C.)

Egyptian civilization developed along the banks of the Nile, in North Africa. Egypt was controlled by an absolute ruler, called the **pharaoh**. Egyptians considered the pharaoh to be a god. Priests, nobles, warriors, scribes, merchants, and craftsmen occupied the middle rungs of Egyptian society. At the bottom of society were peasants and slaves who spent their time farming, herding cattle, and working on massive building projects for the pharaoh. The Egyptians were known for their magnificent stone palaces, temples, and statues. Egyptians believed in life after death. They buried their pharaohs in large tombs called **pyramids**, with gold, jewels and other precious objects for use in the afterlife. The Egyptians also developed their own form of picture writing, called **hieroglyphics**. Hieroglyphics appeared on buildings and on scrolls of paper known as papyrus.

INDUS RIVER VALLEY (2500 B.C.- 1500 B.C.)

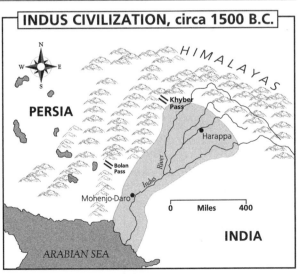

The Indus River Valley was another important center of civilization, arising more than 5,000 years ago. As in Egypt and Mesopotamia, a river deposited rich soil on the plain during its annual flood. Food surpluses allowed people to build cities like Harappa and Mohenjo-Daro. Each had more than 30,000 people. Remarkably, there were public sewers and a water supply. The Indus River peoples were the first to make cotton cloth. It is unclear why this civilization suddenly declined.

THE HUANG HE (2000 B.C.- 1027 B.C.)

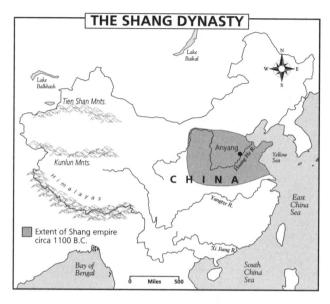

About four thousand years ago, some 500 years after the Harappans settled in the Indus River Valley, China's first civilization developed around the **Huang He** *(Yellow River)*. About 1700 B.C., a **dynasty** *(ruling family)* known as the **Shang** took control. Under the Shang, Chinese craftsmen became skilled at making bronze objects and other crafts. The Chinese discovered how to make silk from silkworm cocoons, constructed irrigation systems, and developed a precise calendar. They also developed their own picture writing, as the ancient Egyptians and Sumerians had done.

OTHER EARLY CIVILIZATIONS

Other early civilizations followed the pattern of the first river valley civilizations — food surpluses, cities, writing, and trade — as well as developing some unique features:

Civilization	Location	Unique Features
Kush	South of Egypt	Kush was influenced by Egyptian culture. Caravans traveled to Kush to obtain iron spears, ivory, and ebony.
Phoenicia	Present-day Lebanon	Phoenicians were outstanding sailors. They also developed the first alphabet. Our modern alphabet is partially based on Phoenician letters.
Hebrew	Present-day Israel	The Hebrews *(Jews)* believed in only one God *(**monotheism**)*. Judaism has a moral code called the **Ten Commandments**, which Jews believe God gave to their leader, **Moses**.

SUMMARIZING YOUR UNDERSTANDING

The Regents will test your understanding of the fifteen themes listed on page 12. Each content chapter will conclude with a brief summary, like this page, identifying:

- **An Overarching Theme**. This theme will identify an important generalization relating not only to the chapter but to all of global history and geography. These themes will often form the basis for thematic essay questions on the Regents Examination.

- **Major Ideas** of the period covered in the chapter. These are classified according to the fifteen themes, which will help you to relate specific examples to general themes.

OVERARCHING THEME

The physical setting of an area affects the development of its culture.

MAJOR IDEAS

GEOGRAPHY
- There is a close relationship between a people's culture and their physical environment.
- The earliest civilizations developed in and near river valleys.

CHANGE
- The Neolithic Revolution and the emergence of the first civilizations were major turning points in history.

POLITICAL SYSTEMS
- People have made different assumptions about power, authority, and law across time and place.

SCIENCE AND TECHNOLOGY
- Technological and scientific advances have helped humankind to meet its basic needs and wants.

IMPORTANT TERMS, CONCEPTS, AND PEOPLE

✦ Neolithic Revolution	✦ Code of Hammurabi	✦ Shang Dynasty
✦ River Valley Civilizations	✦ Pharaoh	✦ Moses
✦ Mesopotamia	✦ Hieroglyphics	✦Ten Commandments

TESTING YOUR UNDERSTANDING

1 In its broadest sense, the term "culture" refers to
   1 art museums and symphony orchestras
   2 the complex languages that are used by developing societies
   3 a centralized form of government that organizes and directs the economy
   4 a distinct way of living and behaving by members of a society

2 During the Neolithic Revolution, people learned how to
   1 create writing systems   3 build fires
   2 grow food and raise animals   4 make bronze weapons

3 Which heading would be most appropriate on the blank line below?

   I. _____
        A. Code of Hammurabi - Mesopotamians
        B. alphabet - Phoenicians
        C. wheel - Sumerians

   1 Economic changes in the ancient world   3 Contributions of ancient civilizations
   2 Buildings of ancient civilizations   4 Religions of ancient civilizations

4 The river valleys of the Tigris and Euphrates, the Nile, and the Indus became early
   centers of civilization because they
   1 had rich deposits of iron ore and coal   3 had rich soils from annual floods
   2 were isolated from other cultures   4 were easy to defend from invasion

5 Our modern-day alphabet is based in large part on the alphabet of the ancient
   1 Phoenicians   3 Egyptians
   2 Chinese   4 Sumerians

6 Cuneiform and hieroglyphics are similar in that they were both
   1 religious temples   3 holy books of ancient Egypt
   2 inventions of the Chinese 4 written forms of communication

7 Judaism differed from other ancient religions in that its followers
   1 worshipped many gods   3 followed the Code of Hammurabi
   2 were monotheists   4 buried their rulers in pyramids

Base your answer to question 8 on the box below and your knowledge of global history.

> • living in cities
> • having a form of writing
> • being skilled at science and technology

8   The above examples are the essential characteristics of a
  1 civilization   3 time period
  2 culture   4 political system

9   Which statement about Egyptian civilization is an *opinion* rather than a historical fact?
  1 The Egyptians had a written language.
  2 Ancient Egypt was protected from invasion by the surrounding desert.
  3 Egyptians produced the most beautiful arts works in the ancient world.
  4 The pyramids were tombs for the pharaohs.

THEMATIC ESSAY QUESTION

Directions: Write a well-organized essay that includes an introduction, several paragraphs explaining your position, and a conclusion.

Theme: Change

> The contributions and achievements of ancient civilizations
> have helped to influence and change the world.

Task:

> Choose *two* ancient civilizations from your study of global history and geography.
>
> For *each* civilization:
> • Describe a contribution or achievement of that civilization.
> • Explain how that contribution or achievement helped to influence and change the world.

You may use any example from your study of global history and geography. Some suggestions you might wish to consider include: Mesopotamia, Egypt, the Indus River Valley Civilizations, and the Huang He Civilization.

You are *not* limited to these suggestions.

CHAPTER 5

THE CLASSICAL CIVILIZATIONS, 500 B.C. to 500 A.D.

During this era, civilizations spread beyond river valleys. Some societies created giant empires. As civilizations began to reflect more on morality and the purpose of life, some of the world's major religions emerged. These civilizations developed institutions, systems of thought, and cultures that still influence us today. As a result, we refer to them as the *classical* civilizations, meaning that they were of the highest class or rank.

Ruins of the Forum, center of politics and commerce in ancient Rome

---

AN OVERVIEW OF CLASSICAL CIVILIZATIONS

- The **Persian Empire** was the first to unite many civilizations, establishing a pattern for future empires.

- The **Greeks** applied reason to inquire about nature and the human condition, laying the foundation for much of Western culture.

- The **Romans** spread Greek culture throughout Western Europe, and left a legacy of language, a system of laws, and Christianity.

- **China** saw the emergence of great philosophers, who set the tone for much of Chinese thought and tradition.

- **India** witnessed a flowering of Hindu and Buddhist cultures, which spread throughout much of South and Southeast Asia.

In studying this era, you should focus on the following questions:

✦ What was the importance of military power, technology and transportation to the development of large empires like Persia, China, and Rome?

✦ What factors led to the collapse of classical civilizations?

✦ How did religion and belief systems influence behavior in this period?

CLASSICAL CIVILIZATIONS OF THE WEST

Three great civilizations dominated the West during this thousand-year period: Persia, Greece, and Rome.

PERSIA

Persia, now known as Iran, is located between Asia and Europe. Beginning around 550 B.C., Persian rulers expanded into other territories, creating the Persian Empire. An **empire** is a state that rules over several different peoples. At its height, the ancient Persian Empire stretched from the Nile to the Indus River.

GREECE

Ancient Greece consisted of a large mountainous peninsula (*mainland Greece*), a large number of islands, and the coast of present-day Turkey. Because most Greek centers of population were separated by mountains and the sea, they developed as independent **city-states**. Although each city-state had its own government, they shared a common culture based on language, religious beliefs, and customs. The two most important city-states were Sparta and Athens.

❖ **Sparta.** Life in Sparta was organized around military needs. Young boys were raised to be disciplined warriors. Strict obedience and self-discipline were highly valued.

❖ **Athens.** Athenians excelled in commerce, and developed a unique form of government by male citizens, known as **democracy** (*rule by the people*). Athenian leaders such as **Pericles** championed the democratic form of government.

THE GOLDEN AGE OF GREECE

In the 5th century B.C., the Greeks enjoyed a "Golden Age" in which art, literature, and philosophy flourished. The Greek ideal of beauty was based on harmony and proportion. Their spirit of free inquiry led to important advances in mathematics and science. Greek sculptures depicted the ideal human form. The Greeks were the first to study philosophy. Their greatest philosophers were **Socrates**, **Plato**, and **Aristotle**.

Rivalry between Athens and Sparta eventually led to the **Peloponnesian War**, in which the Greek city-states fought each other. The Peloponnesian War weakened both Athens and Sparta.

ALEXANDER THE GREAT

In 338 B.C., the king of Macedonia brought all Greek city-states under his control. His son **Alexander the Great** created a vast empire by conquering Egypt, Mesopotamia, and Persia. Alexander extended his conquests as far as the Indus Valley. His conquests helped spread Greek culture and traditions. **Hellenistic culture**, a blend of Greek, Persian, and Egyptian influences, spread throughout the Mediterranean world.

ROME

One of the cultures most affected by ancient Greece was that of Rome. The **Roman Empire** became a major force in the Western world for over 400 years.

The Roman Republic. Early Rome was a city-state located in the center of Italy. It was a **republic** (*a country ruled by elected representatives*) with two main social classes: **patricians** (*wealthy landowners*) and **plebeians** (*craftsmen, merchants, and farmers*). The patricians ruled Rome through the Senate and Consuls. The **Twelve Tables of Roman Law** established a system of written laws to protect the plebeians. Rome gradually conquered other areas, and dominated all of the Mediterranean world by 146 B.C.

The Roman Empire. The Roman general **Julius Caesar** conquered much of Spain and France. When he threatened to seize absolute power in Rome in 44 B.C., he was assassinated. His nephew **Augustus** became the first Roman emperor. Augustus began a long period of peace known as the **Pax Romana**. Rome's centralized political authority, trained officials, and traditions of law allowed it to govern a vast empire. The Romans built public baths, stadiums, temples, aqueducts, and a vast network of roads throughout their empire. Roman concepts of law, engineering, and the Latin language left a rich legacy for the future. However, Romans expected their subjects to worship the emperor as divine. When Jews and Christians refused, they were persecuted.

The Fall of the Roman Empire. In the third century A.D., the Roman Empire was under constant attack by fierce tribes from Northern Europe and Central Asia. Rome also had economic problems. Emperor **Diocletian** attempted to reverse the decline by dividing the empire in two. The eastern empire was ruled from Constantinople (*now Istanbul, in Turkey*), and the western empire was ruled from Rome. In the eastern empire, **Emperor Constantine** converted to Christianity, which later became the official religion. Starting in the late 300s, Huns from Central Asia invaded the western empire, pushing the Germanic tribes forward. By 476 A.D., invaders had burned estates, seized lands, and sacked the city of Rome. The western empire collapsed.

THE CLASSICAL CIVILIZATIONS OF INDIA AND CHINA

INDIA

About 1500 B.C., Aryans, a tribe from Central Asia, invaded the fertile river plains of India. They brought their own religion, known as **Hinduism**. The Aryan conquest also led to the development of the **caste system**, dividing Indians into rigid social classes. Under the caste system, one could only perform certain jobs based on one's caste, and could not marry outside the caste. **Untouchables** were considered below all the other groups, and performed the lowliest tasks in the community.

About 500 B.C., a new religion emerged in India known as **Buddhism**. King **Asoka**, ruler of the **Mauryan Empire** in northern India, converted from Hinduism to Buddhism. Asoka was a tolerant ruler who improved roads, built hospitals, and sent missionaries throughout his empire to spread Buddhism. After the fall of the Mauryan Empire, the **Gupta Empire** arose. This ushered in a "Golden Age" of Hindu culture. Gupta emperors built universities and supported literature and the arts. Gupta mathematicians developed the concepts of zero and infinity, and a decimal system.

CHINA

During the twelve centuries from 1027 B.C., to 220 A.D., China was governed by three dynasties:

DYNASTY	SIGNIFICANCE
Zhou (1027 B.C.-221 B.C.)	Zhou rulers claimed to govern with the **Mandate of Heaven**: heaven would support good rulers and overthrow bad ones. Future rulers used this mandate to justify their authority. The ideas of two Zhou philosophers, **Confucius** and **Lao-zu**, greatly influenced later Chinese history.
Qin (221 B.C.-206 B.C.)	**Shih Huang-ti** overthrew the Zhou and began the Qin dynasty. He was the first Chinese ruler to call himself "emperor." He helped create the **Great Wall of China**, protecting China from invaders to the northwest. His harsh rule led to the collapse of the dynasty after his death.
Han (206 B.C.-220 A.D.)	Han emperors ruled China for the next 400 years. They established examinations to select the best candidates for government service. Merchants traded silk, iron, and bronze along the **Silk Road**, which connected China with the Middle East and Rome.

MAJOR RELIGIONS OF THE CLASSICAL ERA

Several major world religions emerged during the classical era.

HINDUISM

Hindus believe in many gods, all of which are manifestations of a single Supreme Being. They believe in **reincarnation**, meaning that after death a person's soul is reborn as another person or living thing. Those who lead a good life are reborn into a higher caste. Those who do not are reborn into a lower caste or as an animal. Hindus believe that cows are sacred. The Ganges River is also sacred to followers of Hinduism.

BUDDHISM

An Indian Prince, **Siddhartha Gautama**, was the founder of Buddhism. He came to believe that human desires caused all human suffering, and that to find inner peace one must renounce all desires. Gautama became known as the **Buddha**, meaning the "Enlightened One." To give up desires, Buddhists follow the **Eightfold Path**, in which they give up all wealth, meditate, and respect all living things. Following the Eightfold Path helps a person to escape the cycle of continuous reincarnation and to achieve **nirvana**, a state of absolute peace and happiness. Eventually Buddhism spread from India to China, Japan, and Southeast Asia.

CONFUCIANISM

Confucius lived in a time of civil war and disruption in Zhou China. He founded a philosophy based on respecting traditional ways and meeting one's social obligations. Confucius placed great emphasis on the family. He also taught that rulers should govern for the benefit of their subjects, while subjects should obey their ruler. Confucius believed these practices would maintain social peace and harmony.

CHRISTIANITY

Christians believe that **Jesus Christ** was the son of God and sacrificed himself to save humankind from punishment for their sins. Christians believe that after his death, Jesus was resurrected and then rose to Heaven. Jesus' followers, known as the **Apostles**, helped to spread the new Christian religion. Over the centuries, Christianity became the dominant religion in Europe. The Bishop of Rome, known as the **Pope**, exerted control over Western Christendom *(the Roman Catholic Church)*.

SUMMARIZING YOUR UNDERSTANDING

OVERARCHING THEME

*A people's belief system plays a major role
in shaping their history and culture.*

MAJOR IDEAS

INTERDEPENDENCE

- Africa, Asia, and Europe moved in the direction of forming a single world of human interchange in this era as a result of trade, migration, empire-building, missionary activity, and the diffusion of skills and ideas.

CULTURAL AND INTELLECTUAL LIFE

- The application of reason to solving problems has had a dominant influence on Western culture.
- The classical civilizations established institutions and defined values and styles that continue to influence us to this day.

CHANGE

- Both internal and external forces led to the collapse of the Roman Empire

POLITICAL SYSTEMS

- The system of democracy, first developed in ancient Athens, has had a dynamic impact on both Western and other cultures.

IMPORTANT TERMS, CONCEPTS, AND PEOPLE

- ✦ Empire
- ✦ Sparta
- ✦ Athens
- ✦ Golden Age of Greece
- ✦ Peloponnesian Wars
- ✦ Pericles
- ✦ Alexander the Great
- ✦ Hellenistic Culture
- ✦ Roman Empire

- ✦ 12 Tables of Roman Law
- ✦ Augustus
- ✦ Diocletian
- ✦ Pax Romana
- ✦ Constantine
- ✦ Hinduism
- ✦ Caste System
- ✦ King Asoka
- ✦ Buddhism

- ✦ Siddhartha Gautama
- ✦ Reincarnation
- ✦ Eightfold Path
- ✦ Nirvana
- ✦ Gupta Empire
- ✦ Mandate of Heaven
- ✦ Confucius
- ✦ Lao-zu
- ✦ Christianity

TESTING YOUR UNDERSTANDING

1   In both ancient Babylon and the Roman Republic, an important feature of life was the development of
    1 a codified system of laws   3 social and political equality for all
    2 aqueducts to provide water   4 a willingness to accept Christianity

Base your answer to question 2 on the pie chart and your knowledge of global history.

2   Which is a valid conclusion based on the information in the chart?
    1 Athens was a military dictatorship.
    2 Life in Athens was based on the ideal of devotion to an absolute ruler.
    3 Athens was a limited democracy, granting only some citizens the right to vote.
    4 The majority of people in Athens had the right to vote.

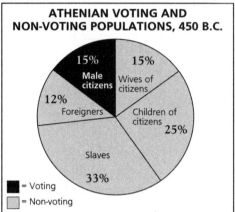

ATHENIAN VOTING AND NON-VOTING POPULATIONS, 450 B.C.

15% Male citizens
15% Wives of citizens
12% Foreigners
Children of citizens 25%
Slaves 33%
■ = Voting
▢ = Non-voting

3   Among the greatest contributions of classical Greek and Roman civilization to world culture were
    1 the first alphabet   3 the decimal system
    2 monotheistic religion   4 innovations in government and law

4   Ancient Egyptian, Greek, and Roman civilizations were all similar in that each
    1 failed to develop a system of writing   3 established industrial economies
    2 controlled neighboring peoples   4 adopted democratic political systems

5   The political system of the Roman Empire was characterized by
    1 strong central government
    2 rule by religious leaders
    3 universal suffrage in national elections
    4 national examinations in philosophy and religion

6   The religions of Judaism and Christianity share a common belief in
    1 nirvana   3 reincarnation
    2 monotheism   4 meditation

7   "By nature men are pretty much alike; it is learning and practice that set them apart."

— *Confucius*

This statement suggests that human differences in the world are mostly due to

1 physical appearances
2 upbringing and experience

3   emotions and feelings
4   inherited characteristics

8   Base your answer to question 8 on the photograph below and on your knowledge of social studies.

Pitlik Collection

Which statement best explains the primary reason why this structure was built?

1 China sought to protect itself from outside invaders.
2 Dynastic rulers wanted to display their grandeur through monumental architecture.
3 China wanted to build a highway to other civilizations.
4 The rulers of China sought to prevent peasants from escaping.

THEMATIC ESSAY QUESTION

Directions: Write a well-organized essay that includes an introduction, several paragraphs explaining your position, and a conclusion.

Theme: Belief Systems

> A people's beliefs often play a major role in shaping their history and culture.

Task:

Choose *two* belief systems from your study of global history and geography.

For *each* belief system:
- Describe two basic beliefs of that religion or philosophy.
- Explain how that religion or philosophy had an impact on a people's history or culture.

You may use any example from your study of global history and geography. Some suggestions you might consider include: Judaism, Greek mythology or philosophy, Christianity, Confucianism, Hinduism, and Buddhism.

You are *not* limited to these suggestions.

DOCUMENT-BASED ESSAY QUESTION

This task is based on the accompanying documents (1-6). Some of these documents have been edited for the purposes of this task. This task is designed to test your ability to work with historical documents. As you analyze the documents, take into account both the source of each document and the author's point of view.

Directions: Read the documents in Part A and answer the questions after each document. Then read the directions for Part B and write your essay.

Historical Context:

We owe a great debt to ancient civilizations. The following documents focus on some of the achievements of ancient civilizations.

Task:

Discuss some of the achievements of ancient civilizations that still influence us today.

Part A — Short Answer

Directions: Analyze the documents and answer the questions that follow each document.

Document 1:

If a son strikes his father, they shall cut off his hand.
If a seignior (*person of rank, like a lord*) destroys the eye of a member of the aristocracy, they shall destroy his eye.
If he knocks out a tooth of a seignior of his own rank, they shall knock out his tooth.
If he knocks out a commoner's tooth, he shall pay one-third mina (*amount*) of silver.
— *Code of Hammurabi,* 1750 B.C.

1. What was the significance of the Code of Hammurabi? _____

Document 2:

Selected letters from the Phoenician alphabet:
   Ϗ [A]   Ⅎ [E]   ↓ [K]   + [T]   O [O]

2. How did the Phoenician alphabet differ from earlier forms of writing? _____

Document 3:

1. I am the Lord your God. You shall have no other Gods before me.
2. You shall not make an idol *(image of a God)*. You shall not bow down to them or worship them.
3. You shall not make wrongful use of the name of the Lord your God.
4. Remember the Sabbath and keep it holy.
5. Honor your father and mother.
6. You shall not kill.
7. You shall not commit adultery.
8. You shall not steal.
9. You shall not bear false witness against your neighbor.
10. You shall not covet anything that belongs to your neighbor.

        — *The Ten Commandments,* from the Hebrew Bible

3. Which of these commandments indicates monotheism? _____

Document 4:

INDIVIDUAL	ACCOMPLISHMENT
Socrates	He challenged Athenians to question basic assumptions and to examine their own conduct to see if they were leading moral lives.
Plato	He extended Socrates' method of questioning to all areas of human knowledge. In his book *The Republic*, he described an ideal society.
Aristotle	An observer of nature, he classified and analyzed plants and animals. He was the "father" of several disciplines, including physics and logic.
Archimedes	He was the first person to make a proof for the area of a circle, to explain the principles of levers, and to measure specific gravity.
Erathosthenes	He computed the circumference of the Earth *(the distance around it)* to within 200 miles.
Euclid	He organized the study of geometry into vigorous logical proofs. His "elements" are still taught today.
Pythagoras	He developed the theorem that the square of the hypotenuse of a right triangle equals the sum of the squares of the other two sides.

4. What does this chart show about Greek ways of thinking? _____

Document 5:

> "Our constitution does not copy the laws of neighboring states. Instead, others copy what we do. Our plan of government favors the many instead of the few; that is why it is called a democracy. As for laws, we offer equal justice to everyone. As for social standing, advancement is open to everyone, according to ability. High position does not depend on wealth."
>
> — *Pericles' Funeral Oration*, Athens, 5th century B.C.

5. In what ways did Pericles indicate that the government of Athens was innovative?

_____

Document 6:

6. Name the person portrayed in the statue, and list a religious belief that his followers spread throughout Asia.

_____

_____

Part B — Essay

Directions:
- Write a well-organized essay that includes an introduction, several paragraphs, and a conclusion.
- Use evidence from the documents to support your response.
- Do not simply repeat the contents of the documents.
- Include specific related information.

Task: Using information from the documents and your knowledge of global history and geography, write an essay in which you:

Discuss some of the achievements of ancient civilizations
that still influence us today.

ANALYZING THE DOCUMENTS

Use the answers you wrote after each document to help you complete the Analysis Box below. The first document and some related outside information have been provided for you. Complete the rest of the Analysis Box. Remember, when analyzing a document you must relate it to the topic.

— ANALYSIS BOX —

Document	Main Idea	Contribution
1. **Code of Hammurabi**	*This is the earliest known written code of laws. It consists of a list of crimes and their punishments. Punishments were based on social class: if a noble knocked out the tooth of a noble, his own tooth was knocked out, but if he knocked out the tooth of a commoner, he only paid a fine.*	*Our society today is also based on written laws.*
2. **Phoenician Alphabet**		
3. **Ten Commandments**		
4. **Greek Contributions**		
5. **Pericles**		
6. **Buddha statue**		

Analyze these documents

Related outside information:
- *The first civilizations began in river valleys.*
- *The ancient Sumerians developed the first known sailboats and the wheel.*
-
-

← Add related information

WRITING THE ANSWER

Now you should be ready to write your essay. The opening sentences and the first part of the essay have been written for you. Complete the other parts of the essay. Use the information in your Analysis Box as a guide.

①
The opening sentence gives the historical context.

②
The second sentence is the topic statement.

③
A transition sentence introduces the specific examples you are going to relate to the topic statement.

④
Your second paragraph should discuss an example supporting the topic statement. Write the information from the document in your own words.

⑤
Outside information related to the example is added here.

⑥
This sentence ties the document to the topic: that ancient civilizations influence us today.

⑦
Your next three paragraphs should discuss other examples supporting the topic statement. Be sure to tie in other documents or outside information related to the example.

⑧
Your closing paragraph should restate the topic statement and refer to your examples (in this case, writing, law, science and philosophy, and religion).

The first civilizations began in river valleys — the Nile, the Indus, and the Tigris and Euphrates — and gradually spread to other regions. The achievements of these ancient civilizations still influence us today. They can be seen in at least four areas: writing, law, science and philosophy, and religion.

Ancient civilizations developed the first writing systems. Document 2 shows some letters from the Phoenician alphabet. Earlier writing systems — hieroglyphics, cuneiform, and Chinese characters — had thousands of symbols, while the Phoenician alphabet had a small number of symbols, each representing a particular sound. With just a few symbols, it was easier to learn to read and write. In time, their alphabet evolved into the alphabet we use in English today.

A second area in which ancient civilizations influence us today is the law. For example, _____

_____

_____

A third area in which ancient civilizations influence us today is in science and philosophy. For example, _____

_____

_____

A fourth area in which ancient civilizations influence us today is in religion. For example, _____

_____

_____

Therefore, we can see that ancient civilizations laid the foundations for many of our beliefs and ways of doing things. These range from written languages and religions to our system of laws, and scientific and philosophical knowledge.

Note: Another practice document-based essay question is included in Chapter 9.

CHAPTER 6

NEW CENTERS OF CULTURE IN AN AGE OF TURMOIL, 500 - 1200 A.D.

In the late 400s, much of the world entered a period of turmoil. After the Roman and Han empires fell, four regions of the world experienced great changes:

CHANGES AFTER THE FALL OF ROME AND THE COLLAPSE OF THE HAN DYNASTY

- **Byzantium**. The eastern part of the Roman Empire became known as the Byzantine Empire, and continued for another 1,000 years. It preserved much of Roman and Greek culture and developed its own type of Christianity.

- **Middle East**. A new religion, Islam, appeared in the 7th century. Arab nomads swept across Southwest Asia and North Africa, establishing a new Islamic empire, while absorbing local traditions.

- **Western Europe**. Much of the Greek and Roman heritage was lost. Christianity became the main binding force among Europeans. A new method of social and political organization emerged, known as feudalism.

- **China**. Basic patterns of Chinese culture re-emerged after almost 400 years of civil war. China was also affected by a new religious impulse: Buddhism. Meanwhile, Chinese culture spread to Japan.

In contrast to Western Europe, great centers of culture and urbanization in China, the Islamic world, and Byzantium experienced "Golden Ages" in this period. By the end of this era, the Christian Crusades brought Europeans into greater contact with these societies. In studying this era, you should focus on the following:

Jarrett Archives

✦ What were the main cultural achievements of this era?
✦ What role did major religions play in the events of this period?
✦ What was feudalism, and how did it operate?

Crusaders pray before leaving to do battle in the Holy Land

NEW CENTERS OF CULTURE EMERGE

Although this era followed Rome's collapse in the West, much of the heritage of classical civilization was preserved by the Byzantine and Islamic Empires.

THE BYZANTINE EMPIRE, 330 - 1453 A.D.

Although the western half of the Roman Empire collapsed in the 5th century, the eastern half, known as the **Byzantine Empire**, lasted for another thousand years. The Byzantine emperors ruled from the capital city of Constantinople, with the help of a powerful army and an imperial bureaucracy. **Emperor Justinian** codified Roman laws (**Code of Justinian**) and built a magnificent church, the Hagia Sophia. The Byzantines were greatly influenced by Greek

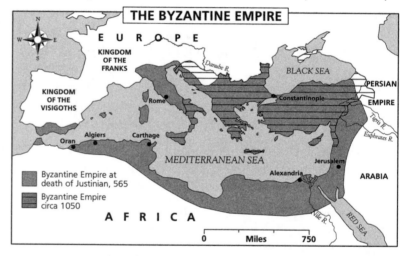

and Roman culture, and in fact spoke mainly Greek. They prospered from their location at a crossroads of trade. The Byzantines developed their own form of Christianity, known as the **Eastern Orthodox Christianity**. The Byzantines controlled Egypt, the Middle East, and Eastern Europe. Gradually the empire declined as it lost territories to its neighbors, especially the Islamic Empire. Constantinople finally fell in 1453.

THE RISE OF THE ISLAMIC EMPIRE

For centuries, overland caravans had carried goods up the western coast of the Arabian peninsula, stopping in oasis towns like **Mecca**. **Mohammed**, an Arab merchant from Mecca, was influenced by Jewish and Christian beliefs. He had a vision commanding him to convert the Arab tribes to belief in a single God, known in Arabic as **Allah**. Mohammed won a large number of followers, but he was driven out of Mecca in 622 A.D. by jealous merchants, and fled to Medina. His supporters retook Mecca in a **jihad** (*holy war*) in 630. The religion he founded is known as **Islam**, and its followers are called **Muslims**.

Mohammed's teachings were recorded in the **Qu'ran** (*Koran*), Islam's holiest book. Muslims follow the **Five Pillars of Faith**: they avow that Allah is the only God and Mohammed is his prophet, pray five times a day while facing Mecca, give to the poor, fast during the holy month of Ramadan, and try to make one pilgrimage to Mecca.

Islam quickly spread from Mecca throughout the Arabian peninsula. The Arab Empire then expanded to Egypt and North Africa, Syria and Persia. Muslim invaders even conquered much of Spain. Influenced by both the Middle East and the achievements of Greece and Rome, the Arabs achieved a **Golden Age** at a time when learning was in a severe decline in Western Europe. Arab scholars studied ancient Greek and Latin texts. They borrowed the concept of zero from India, and developed Arabic numerals. Their craftsmen made beautiful tapestries, leather goods, and carpets.

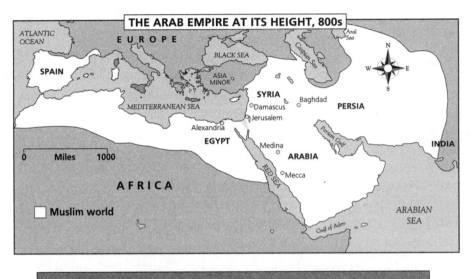

THE ARAB EMPIRE AT ITS HEIGHT, 800s

THE RISE OF FEUDALISM IN EUROPE

While the Byzantine and Arab Empires emerged as new cultural centers, important changes were occurring in Western Europe. Romans considered those peoples outside the boundaries of their empire, such as the Germanic tribes, as "barbarians." Eventually, these barbarians invaded Rome and established their own kingdoms throughout Western Europe. The constant migration and warfare of this period caused Rome's central government to collapse and disrupted trade. People abandoned cities and lost interest in learning. Only priests and a few others could read and write. Historians refer to this era of European history, from the fall of Rome to the 1400s, as the **Middle Ages** or **Medieval** period.

CHARLEMAGNE AND THE FRANKS

The Franks eventually established the largest of the new Germanic kingdoms. **Charlemagne** became king of the Franks in 768. He expanded the Frankish practice of giving land to his nobles in exchange for their promises of loyalty and service. His nobles then gave land to those below them in exchange for similar promises. Peasants put themselves in service to their local lords for security. Charlemagne expanded the Frankish kingdom while resisting Islamic expansion. He also encouraged learning by establishing church schools. Although his empire did not last beyond his death, Charlemagne established the social, cultural, and political foundations for much of Western Europe over the next several centuries.

FEUDAL SOCIETY IN EUROPE

The system established by the Franks became known as **feudalism** — a social and political system in which the king relied on the services of loyal nobles. Feudalism spread through Europe as a way to defend landholdings and meet basic economic needs. Feudal society was divided into rulers, nobles, knights, and serfs. **Serfs** were peasants who were bound to the lands of their lord *(local knight or noble)*. The lord lived in a manor house, surrounded by his farmland. The **manor** produced its own food, clothing, and other supplies. Serfs gave the lord part of their harvest and other services in exchange for use of his land. The lord had almost absolute power over the serfs on his manor.

ROLE OF THE CHURCH IN FEUDAL EUROPE

Religious life was controlled by the **Catholic Church**, which had survived the barbarian invasions. It was the single most important organization in Western Europe during the Middle Ages. It was the main center of learning. Even more important, most Europeans were deeply religious and believed that the Church represented God on Earth, with the power to send people to heaven or hell when they died.

The power of the Church was demonstrated by the **Crusades**. In the 11th Century, Seljuk Turks conquered Jerusalem and drove out Christian pilgrims. The Pope was outraged, and organized a force of Christian rulers and nobles from across Europe to reconquer the "Holy Land." Seven Crusades went forth over two centuries. Although Jerusalem was not permanently reconquered, the Crusades gave Europeans greater exposure to Arab scholarship, such as Arab-translated Greek and Roman texts and the use of zero, as well as to Asian goods such as silk, spices, coffee, cotton cloth, and glass mirrors. The Crusaders whetted Europeans' appetite for foreign goods, but also led to religious intolerance. Christians persecuted Muslims and Jews, and Muslims persecuted Christians.

THE GOLDEN AGES OF CHINA AND JAPAN

T'ANG AND SUNG CHINA

Like Western Europe, China endured a long period of unrest after the Han Dynasty collapsed in 220 A.D. This unrest ended with the rise of the **T'ang Dynasty** (618-907). T'ang rulers reunited China and brought on a new "Golden Age." Architecture, painting, sculpture, and Confucian philosophy flourished.

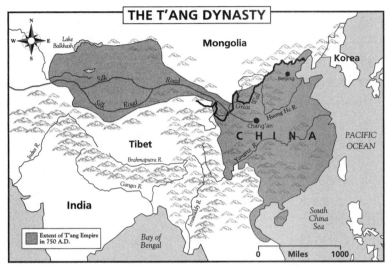

The **Sung Dynasty** (960-1279) replaced the T'ang in the 10th century. Sung China was the most populous and advanced civilization of its day. Chinese artists perfected making porcelain and painting on silk paper. Sung China made many important inventions and discoveries that later influenced other cultures, including gunpowder, the crossbow, and the compass.

JAPAN'S GOLDEN AGE: THE HEIAN PERIOD

China greatly influenced Japanese diet, government, writing, and art. Nonetheless, Japan was not a "copy" of China. The Japanese followed the **Shinto** religion. They believed their emperor was descended from the Sun Goddess and did not accept the Chinese view of the Mandate of Heaven. Japanese nobles did not adopt China's examination system, which created opportunities for commoners to enter government service.

During the **Heian Period,** leading nobles spent much of their time at the emperor's court. Art and literature flourished. **Lady Murasaki** wrote *The Tale of Genji,* one of the earliest known novels. By the end of the Heian Period, many noble landowners began to raise their own armies of warriors, known as **samurai.** The imperial government weakened and was unable to prevent nobles from fighting one another for land and power.

SUMMARIZING YOUR UNDERSTANDING

OVERARCHING THEME

Human progress has been achieved through both continuity and change.

MAJOR IDEAS

CHANGE

- A society's culture often changes when it comes into contact with the cultures of other societies, such as when Romans encountered "barbarians" or Christians encountered Muslims.

BELIEF SYSTEMS

- During this era, Buddhism, Christianity, Hinduism, and Islam spread far and wide beyond their lands of origin.
- In the Middle Ages, people's ideas were greatly influenced by their religious beliefs.

DIVERSITY

- Centuries of warfare between Byzantines and Muslims, followed by the Crusades, demonstrated that religious differences often lead to conflict.
- In this era there was no contact between the Americas and the rest of the world. As a result the people of the Americas did not share in the cultural exchanges that stimulated innovation of all kinds in Europe, Asia, and Africa.

GEOGRAPHY

- The example of China shows that geographic isolation can promote cultural unity, but can also bring about political isolation.

MOVEMENT

- Contacts between Christians and Muslims stimulated trade and introduced new ideas to Europe.

IMPORTANT TERMS, CONCEPTS, AND PEOPLE

- ✦ Byzantine Empire
- ✦ Code of Justinian
- ✦ Islam
- ✦ Qu'ran
- ✦ Mohammed

- ✦ Five Pillars of Faith
- ✦ Charlemagne
- ✦ Middle Ages
- ✦ Feudalism
- ✦ Manors

- ✦ Crusades
- ✦ T'ang Dynasty
- ✦ Sung Dynasty
- ✦ Heian Period
- ✦ Samurai

TESTING YOUR UNDERSTANDING

1   An immediate result of the fall of the Roman Empire was
    1 a renewed interest in education and the arts
    2 a period of disorder and lack of central government
    3 the growth of cities and the rise of the middle class
    4 an increase in trade and manufacturing

2   In the Roman and Byzantine Empires, an important feature of life was
    1 a body of codified law   3 social and political equality
    2 the Islamic religion   4 civil service examinations

Base your answer to questions 3 and 4 on the passage below and on your knowledge of global history.

3   People who accept the beliefs stated in this passage practice
    1 polytheism   3 emperor worship
    2 monotheism   4 animism

> **IN THE NAME OF ALLAH**
> **THE COMPASSIONATE, THE MERCIFUL**
> Praise be to Allah, Lord of the Creation,
> The Compassionate, the Merciful,
> King of the last Judgment!
> You alone we worship,
>   and to You we pray for help

4   In which book can this passage be found?
    1 Old Testament   3 Talmud
    2 Analects of Confucius   4 Qu'ran

5   The Middle Ages in Europe were characterized by
    1 the manor system and feudal ties
    2 absolute monarchies and strong central governments
    3 decreased emphasis on religion in daily life
    4 extensive trade with East Asia and the Middle East

6   Which is the most valid generalization about the Crusades?
    1 They strengthened the power of the serfs in Europe.
    2 They stimulated a desire for increased trade between Europe and Asia.
    3 They brought European influence to Africa.
    4 They promoted the idea of religious freedom.

7   Feudal societies are generally characterized by
    1 an exchange of land for services   3 widespread economic opportunity
    2 representative government   4 the protection of individual rights

8 Which statement best describes the role of the Roman Catholic Church in Europe during the Middle Ages?
1 The Church encouraged individuals to question authority.
2 Church leaders were involved solely in spiritual activities.
3 The Church gained in influence as the world became more secular.
4 The Church provided a sense of stability, unity, and order.

9 One factor accounting for Chinese influence on traditional Japanese culture was the
1 continuous warfare between the two countries
2 geographic proximity of the two countries
3 refusal of Western nations to trade with Japan
4 annexation of Japan by the Chinese Empire

10 The traditional Japanese concept of the role of the emperor and the Chinese idea of the Mandate of Heaven were both based on
1 the democratic election of rulers
2 a division of power between the nobility and the emperor
3 a belief that political power comes from a divine source
4 a constitution that protected individual rights

THEMATIC ESSAY QUESTION

Directions: Write a well-organized essay that includes an introduction, several paragraphs explaining your position, and a conclusion.

Theme: Cultural and Intellectual Life

> Throughout history, many cultures have experienced a "Golden Age."

Task:

> Choose *two* cultures from your study of global history and geography.
>
> For *each* culture:
> * Describe two achievements of that culture's "Golden Age."
> * Discuss one way in which the two cultures are similar or different.

You may use any example from your study of global history and geography. Some suggestions you may wish to consider include: Athens (5th Century B.C.), Gupta Dynasty, Islamic world (700s-1100s), T'ang Dynasty, and Heian Period.
You are *not* limited to these suggestions.

CHAPTER 7

WARRIORS ON HORSEBACK AND THE REVIVAL OF EUROPE, 1200 - 1500

From 1200 to 1500, separate civilizations continued along their own unique paths of development but became more influenced by one another than ever before. As trade increased and ideas spread, the cultures of Europe, Asia, and Africa became more connected. These were also times of great stress. Nomadic invaders from Central Asia were greatly feared by neighboring civilizations. The Bubonic Plague, a deadly disease from Central Asia, brought devastation in the 1300s.

OVERVIEW OF THE PERIOD FROM 1200 TO 1500

- **West Africa.** Important empires prospered from their trade in gold and salt.

- **Asia.** Mongol warriors swept across the Asian mainland, uniting much of Asia under their rule.

- **Japan.** Japan developed a political and social system very similar to feudalism in Western Europe.

- **Europe.** Europe had a rebirth of trade and learning. These developments led to the end of feudalism and the achievements of the Renaissance.

During these centuries, Islamic civilization continued to grow. What was left of the Byzantine Empire collapsed. In studying this era, you should focus on the following:

✦ What led to the rise of the West African kingdoms?

✦ What were the effects of the Mongol conquests?

✦ What factors contributed to the decline of feudalism in Western Europe?

✦ What were the achievements of the European Renaissance?

A gold pendant from the Kingdom of Mali

Smithsonian Institution

THE KINGDOMS OF AFRICA

Much of North Africa is occupied by the **Sahara Desert.** Just below it is a wide band of grassland called the **savanna.** South of the savanna lie tropical rain forests.

THE WEST AFRICAN KINGDOMS

The Sahara Desert separated the peoples of sub-Saharan Africa from those of North Africa and Eurasia. Nevertheless, merchants on camels crossed the Sahara to trade with West Africans for gold and other riches. At the same time, West Africans needed salt. Merchants picked up blocks of salt along their journey. This thriving **gold-salt trade** gave rise to a series of powerful kingdoms in the West African savanna.

KINGDOM	DESCRIPTION
Ghana 750-1200	The first great West African kingdom was Ghana. Its rulers' power rested on their ability to tax the gold and salt trade passing through the region. The rulers of Ghana built a capital city and developed a large cavalry.
Mali 1240-1400	Mali extended its empire by controlling the gold mines of equatorial Africa. Mali's rulers also adopted Islam. In the 1330s, their ruler **Mansa Musa** made a pilgrimage to Mecca. He brought back Arab scholars and turned the capital city of **Timbuktu** into a center of learning.
Songhai 1464-1600	The people of Songhai later captured Timbuktu and brought the Upper Niger region under their control. Unlike Mali, the common people as well as its rulers adopted Islam. Songhai established its trading network as far as Europe.

OTHER AFRICAN STATES

Benin, famous for its bronze sculptures, developed in the rain forests of West Africa. In the south, **Zimbabwe** flourished near important gold deposits. Its people built massive stone fortifications, and traded gold, copper, and ivory with Arabs along the coast. Other important city-states developed along the east coast of Africa in the 10th century. In northeastern Africa, **Ethiopia** had become a Christian state as early as the 4th century; it remained Christian, even though it was cut off from other Christian states by the rise of Islam.

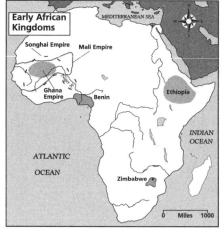

THE WARRIOR STATES OF ASIA

Stretching across Eurasia is an almost unbroken band of dry, treeless grasslands called **steppes**. The steppes provided an environment in which nomadic peoples could herd animals and perfect their horsemanship and fighting skills. For centuries, the Huns, Turks, and Mongols pushed out of this region to conquer their neighbors.

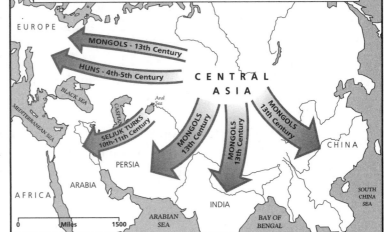

CENTRAL ASIAN INVADERS, 4th to 13th CENTURIES

CHINGGIS KHAN CREATES THE MONGOL EMPIRE

Chinggis (*Ghengis*) **Khan** (1162-1227) united various Mongol tribes and began conquering areas in northern China. In 1219, Chinggis captured the Muslim states of Central Asia. His successors conquered Persia, Russia, and the rest of China — creating one of the largest empires the world has ever seen.

THE YUAN DYNASTY (1279-1368)

The vast Mongol Empire was divided into four kingdoms. **Kublai Khan**, Chinggis' grandson, became ruler of northern China in 1260 and later united all of China. He encouraged the Mongols to adopt Chinese ways and even adopted the Chinese name **Yuan** for his dynasty. **Marco Polo**, an Italian merchant, visited China in the 1270s. He was astonished at the magnificence of the Khan's court and at Chinese technology. Polo's writings aroused great interest about China in Europe. Despite their achievements, the Mongol rulers were greatly resented by the Chinese and were overthrown in 1368.

MONGOL RULE IN RUSSIA

Russia began as an organized state in the 800s. The Slavs founded the first Russian kingdom in Kiev. Later Russian city-states developed at Novogrod and Moscow. Aspects of Byzantine culture, such as Orthodox Christianity and the Cyrillic alphabet, were introduced into Russia. Russian culture became a blend of Slavic and Byzantine traditions. In the 1200s the Mongols conquered Russia, ruling it for almost 200 years. However, in 1480 **Ivan the Great** declared independence from the Mongols for Muscovy (*the region around Moscow*). He declared himself **Tsar** (*emperor*) and conquered neighboring lands, creating the nucleus of modern Russia.

FEUDALISM IN JAPAN

The Mongols never conquered Japan, but by the 1100s the Japanese emperor's power had so weakened that Japan collapsed into civil war. In 1192, one noble family defeated all its rivals and had the emperor appoint its head as **Shogun**. For the next 600 years, the Shoguns were the real rulers of Japan; the emperors were mere figureheads.

Like Europe, the Japanese adopted a system of feudalism. Beneath the Shogun were nobles, known as **Daimyo**. The Daimyo pledged loyalty to the Shogun and provided him with the services of **samurai**. Samurai warriors followed a strict code of honor known as **Bushido**, which emphasized loyalty to the Daimyo. Farmers, merchants, and artisans were at the bottom of the social scale.

By the 1200s, the Shogun's power weakened, and the Daimyo were able to rule their own lands with little government interference. Despite constant fighting between rival Daimyo, this period saw the birth of such traditional Japanese arts as landscape painting, the tea ceremony, flower arranging, and gardening. Each of these art forms reflected the beauty of nature and the importance of calm spiritual enlightenment.

RENAISSANCE AND REFORMATION IN EUROPE

THE DECLINE OF FEUDALISM

Beginning in the 1200s, increased trade led to the growth of towns and guilds, the rise of the middle class, and the greater use of money in Europe. In the late 1300s, rats with fleas carrying the **Bubonic Plague** (known as the **Black Death)** entered Europe from Asia on trading ships. Between 1347 and 1351, one-third of Europe's population died in the epidemic. This caused labor shortages, and peasants were able to escape from serfdom when landowners offered them freedom in exchange for work. Other serfs escaped to the towns, where they became free laborers. Gunpowder began to be used for cannons and muskets, and knights became vulnerable to soldiers with firearms. Kings with large armies gained power over their nobles. Next, the rise of cities, the growth of trade, the decline of knights, the emergence of powerful kings, and the collapse of serfdom gradually ended the old feudal order in Western Europe.

THE RENAISSANCE

The **Renaissance** was a period of great intellectual and artistic activity that began in Italy in the 1400s and gradually spread to the rest of Europe. Situated between Europe and Asia, Italian cities such as Florence and Venice had grown rich from the East-West trade. Italy was also home to many classical ruins from ancient times. Wealthy nobles and merchants acted as patrons supporting artists, writers, and scholars. Renaissance thinkers celebrated the achievements of human reason and the human spirit. They abandoned the focus of the Middle Ages on the life hereafter and showed greater interest in the present world.

Artists developed the technique of perspective to give greater realism to their painting. **Leonardo da Vinci**, **Michelangelo**, and **Raphael** are considered among the greatest artists of all time. There was a growth of **secularism** — looking at the world from a non-religious viewpoint. In his book *The Prince*, **Machiavelli** advised rulers to do whatever was necessary to maintain their power. Scholars like **Galileo** developed the **scientific method** *(using observation and experience to explain the world)*, rather than simply looking to Church teachings. **Copernicus** discovered that the Earth was not the center of the universe, but that it and other planets revolved around the sun.

THE PROTESTANT REFORMATION

The Renaissance spirit of inquiry led to a questioning of widespread abuses within the Catholic Church. In 1517, **Martin Luther** nailed **95 Theses** to a church door in Germany, challenging the Pope's right to sell **indulgences** *(pardons from sin)*. Luther believed that people could find salvation only through personal faith in God. After he was excommunicated, he broke with the Church and began the **Protestant Reformation**. Other reformers, like **John Calvin**, started their own churches. **Johann Gutenberg**'s invention of moveable type for printing helped spread Protestant ideas through books.

THE CATHOLIC COUNTER-REFORMATION

The Reformation shattered the unity of the Catholic Church. **Henry VIII** of England broke with the Pope and made England Protestant in 1534. Catholics fought the spread of Protestantism with the **Counter-Reformation**. They reformed abuses at the **Council of Trent**, introduced the **Inquisition** *(investigating disbelievers in Church teachings)*, and founded the **Jesuits** *(a group dedicated to spreading Catholicism)*. Religious rivalry plunged Europe into a century of war. The **Wars of Religion** led kings to increase their armies and taxes, resulting in a tremendous upsurge in royal power.

SUMMARIZING YOUR UNDERSTANDING

OVERARCHING THEME

*The development of new ideas can lead to
profound political, economic, and social changes.*

MAJOR IDEAS

MOVEMENT OF PEOPLE AND GOODS
- West African empires developed as a result of the gold and salt trade.

GEOGRAPHY
- The Central Asian steppes provided an ideal environment for developing a cavalry.

CHANGE
- The Mongol conquests demonstrated that invasions tend to change the political and cultural institutions of both the conquered and the invader.
- Rulers and social groups sometimes resist social and political change.

CULTURAL AND INTELLECTUAL LIFE
- The Renaissance was based on new ways of thinking, leading to revolutions in astronomy, science, technology, painting, literature, and overseas exploration.
- The Renaissance spirit of inquiry led to a challenge of the authority of the Catholic Church during the Reformation.

IMPORTANT TERMS, CONCEPTS, AND PEOPLE

✦ Timbuktu	✦ Ivan the Great	✦ Protestant Reformation
✦ Mansa Musa	✦ Bushido	✦ Martin Luther
✦ Steppes	✦ Black Death	✦ Ninety-five Theses
✦ Mongols	✦ Renaissance	✦ Counter Reformation
✦ Chinggis Khan	✦ Machiavelli	✦ Council of Trent
✦ Kublai Khan	✦ Leonardo da Vinci	✦ Inquisition
✦ Marco Polo	✦ Michelangelo	✦ Johann Gutenberg

TESTING YOUR UNDERSTANDING

1   One reason the kingdoms of West Africa prospered was that they
    1 were located along the Tigris and Euphrates Rivers
    2 had no contact with the rest of the world
    3 followed the Hindu beliefs of their rulers
    4 developed an extensive trade in gold and salt

2   Why did so many fierce nomadic tribes emerge out of Central Asia?
    1 Warm climates encouraged population growth.
    2 Diseases like the Bubonic Plague drove Central Asians into Europe.
    3 Vast grasslands supported large numbers of warriors on horseback.
    4 The Hindu faith encouraged them to fight.

3   Which was a characteristic of feudalism in both medieval Europe and Japan?
    1 The middle class acquired more power than any other class.
    2 Political power was held by a strong central government.
    3 The army encouraged strong nationalist feelings.
    4 People pledged absolute loyalty to those above them.

4   The fifth century B.C. in Greece, often called the "Golden Age" of Greece, and the Renaissance in Italy were both characterized by
    1 religious revival   3 social and political upheaval
    2 economic decline   4 artistic and literary achievements

5   Which leader unified the Mongol tribes and conquered much of Asia?
    1 Ivan the Terrible   3 Chinggis Khan
    2 Mansa Musa   4 Sunni Ali

6   The sale of indulgences and the behavior of the clergy were the subject of
    1 Lady Murasaki's *The Tale of Genji*   3 Martin Luther's *95 Theses*
    2 William Shakespeare's *Hamlet*   4 Niccolo Machiavelli's *The Prince*

7   "Christians should be taught that one who gives to a poor man or lends to a needy man does better than if he used the money to buy an indulgence."
    This statement was most likely made by
    1 Mansa Musa   3 William Shakespeare
    2 Niccolo Machiavelli   4 Martin Luther

8 One reason Italian city-states were able to dominate trade routes at the beginning of the Renaissance was that they were
  1 located on the Mediterranean Sea
  2 north of the Alps
  3 on the North Sea trade routes
  4 on the Atlantic seaboard

9 Which statement best describes a change that occurred during the Renaissance?
  1 Feudalism became the dominant political system.
  2 The use of reason and logic was discouraged.
  3 People put unquestioning faith in Church teachings.
  4 Observation and experience were used to explain the world more scientifically.

10 The Renaissance and the Protestant Reformation were similar in that both were
  1 stimulated by a spirit of inquiry
  2 supported by the peasantry
  3 limited to Italy and Germany
  4 reactions to the spread of Islam

THEMATIC ESSAY QUESTION

Directions: Write a well-organized essay that includes an introduction, several paragraphs explaining your position, and a conclusion.

Theme: Culture and Intellectual Life

> Art works often express the political, social, and economic conditions of the time period in which they were created.

Task:

Choose *two* works of art from your study of global history and geography.

For *each* work of art:
- Describe the time period in which it was created.
- Describe how the artwork expressed the political, social, or economic conditions of that period.

You may use any example from your study of global history. Some suggestions you may wish to consider include: the pyramids in Egypt, the Parthenon in Athens, the Colosseum in Rome, the porcelain figures of the T'ang and Sung dynasties, the bronze figures of Benin in West Africa, and the Mona Lisa.

You are *not* limited to these suggestions.

CHAPTER 8

THE BIRTH OF THE MODERN WORLD, 1500 - 1770

The centuries from 1500 to 1750 witnessed the birth of the "modern world," with the following important developments:

- a greater awareness of other cultures
- the creation of a global economy
- the rise of powerful nation-states
- major technological advances
- a deepening reliance on science

Library of Congress

Explorers like Magellan helped link Europe to the rest of the world

In this chapter you will read about the impact these developments had on several different areas of the world:

- **The Encounter Between Europe and the Americas**. This encounter brought together the major centers of civilization and created a truly global economy. By creating colonial empires in the Americas and transporting slaves from Africa, Europeans exerted greater power on the world than ever before.

- **Europe in the Age of Kings.** Absolute monarchs formed large armies by taxing new wealth. New challenges to traditional thinking emerged with the Scientific Revolution and the Enlightenment.

- **The Territorial Empires of Asia**. Great empires flourished in the Middle East, Persia, India, and China. Nevertheless, the pace of change in this part of the world fell behind that of Europe.

In studying this era, you should focus on the following questions:

✦ What were the key achievements of the Pre-Columbian civilizations?
✦ How did the European encounter affect Native Americans and Africans?
✦ How did the Scientific Revolution and the Enlightenment change Europe?
✦ What were the main characteristics of the Asian empires from the 1500s to the 1700s?

THE ENCOUNTER BETWEEN EUROPE AND THE AMERICAS

While complex civilizations were flourishing in Europe, Asia, and Africa, equally striking developments had been occurring in the Americas.

THE FIRST AMERICANS

As early as 25,000 years ago, Asian hunters crossed from Siberia to Alaska and migrated throughout North and South America. Between 1500 B.C. and 1200 A.D., several complex Native American civilizations developed in **Mesoamerica** (*present-day Mexico and Central America*) and in South America.

MAJOR NATIVE AMERICAN EMPIRES

MAYA, 1500 B.C.- 1546 A.D. The Maya developed a complex civilization in Guatemala. They built cities with palaces, temples, and pyramids. They also developed a hieroglyphic system of writing, a number system using zero, and a 365-day calendar. About 800 A.D., the Maya migrated to Mexico, where they built cities with stone pyramids as high as modern buildings.

AZTEC, 1200 -1521 A.D. The Aztecs settled in central Mexico around 1300. They learned to grow corn and acquired other skills from their neighbors. Over the next two centuries, they often went to war and conquered neighboring peoples. Captured warriors were frequently sacrificed to the Aztec sun god. Like the Maya, the Aztecs developed a form of writing and an accurate calendar.

INCA, 1200-1353 A.D. The Inca lived along the Pacific coast of South America. By 1400 they ruled an empire extending throughout the Andes mountains. They built stone roads stretching for thousands of miles. Superb engineering skills allowed them to build vast stone buildings high in the Andes. Although they did not develop writing, they used bundles of intricately knotted ropes to keep records and send messages.

THE EUROPEAN "AGE OF DISCOVERY"

A new inquiring spirit, as well as devices like the compass and the moveable rudder, led Europeans to explore the oceans. The conquest of Constantinople by the Ottoman Turks in 1453 cut Europe off from trade with Asia, creating another incentive to find new sea routes to Asia. Several European rulers believed that control of trade with East Asia would bring them vast wealth.

Spain and Portugal led the way in looking for a sea route to East Asia. The Italian sea captain **Christopher Columbus** believed that he could reach Asia by sailing west instead of east. In 1492, he received financial support from the King and Queen of Spain. Instead of reaching Asia, Columbus landed in the Americas. His "discovery" of the Americas provided new sources of wealth for Europe. Meanwhile, the rulers of Portugal sent **Vasco Da Gama** sailing southwards. In 1497, he sailed around the southern tip of Africa and on to India. Da Gama's discovery made it possible for Europeans to reach Asia without taking overland routes. In 1519, **Ferdinand Magellan** led an expedition of ships around the world, confirming that it was round. As a result of these discoveries, other rulers sent out explorers to find new trade routes and to claim ownership of "newly-discovered" lands.

VOYAGES OF EARLY EUROPEAN EXPLORERS

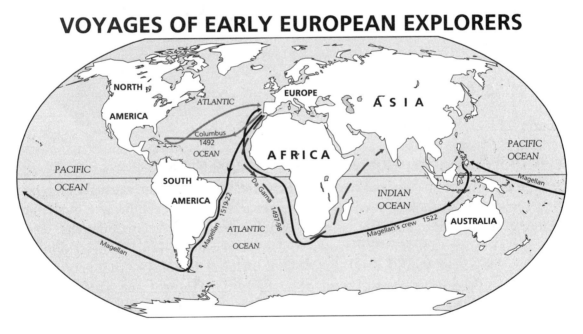

THE EUROPEAN CONQUEST OF THE AMERICAS

The arrival of Europeans had a profound impact on Native Americans. Spanish **conquistadors** arrived in the "New World" soon after the explorers. In 1519, **Hernando Cortés** landed in Mexico with horses, cannons, and several hundred soldiers. Three years later he stormed the Aztec capital. Cortés triumphed partly because he had cannons and horses, but the Aztecs were also worn down by deaths from smallpox and other European diseases against which they had no immunity. By 1533, **Francisco Pizarro** was able to subdue the Inca in South America, who had been weakened by civil war.

EFFECTS OF THE ENCOUNTER

The encounter between Native American and European cultures led to the exchange of ideas, foods, goods, and technologies. Such exchanges are referred to as **cultural diffusion**. The European diet was improved by the introduction of new foods like tomatoes, corn, potatoes, and chocolate. Gold and silver from the Americas and the establishment of overseas colonies enriched Spain and led to a shift in trade routes. New diseases in the Americas killed a large percentage of the Native American population.

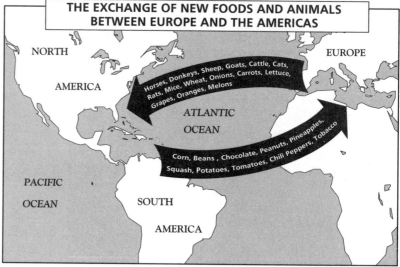

THE COLONIAL EXPERIENCE IN LATIN AMERICA

Spain took control of Mexico, South America, and the Caribbean. Portugal took possession of Brazil. Catholic priests began converting Native Americans to Christianity. European nobles and soldiers set up their own estates, known as **encomiendas**, where Native Americans were forced to work. A new social order developed, headed by European nobles called **Peninsulares**. Below them were the **Creoles** — those born in the Americas of European parents. People of mixed blood, **Mestizos** and **Mulattos**, were slightly above the status of Native Americans and Africans, who were treated as slaves.

THE TRANSATLANTIC SLAVE TRADE

Harsh working conditions and the deaths of many Native Americans from disease created a demand for more workers. Captured Africans were traded to European sea captains and merchants along the coasts of Africa in exchange for guns and other goods. Over the next 300 years, slave traders removed as many as 20 million Africans to the Americas. The Transatlantic slave trade disrupted African culture and encouraged warfare in Africa. It also resulted in cultural diffusion, bringing European firearms and goods to Africa, and African music, legends, and beliefs to the Americas.

EUROPE IN THE AGE OF KINGS, 1600-1770

In Europe the pace of change continued to pick up speed between 1600 and 1770. The Commercial Revolution, Scientific Revolution, and Enlightenment all began in Europe in these years, but had far-ranging impacts on the rest of the world.

THE COMMERCIAL REVOLUTION

The **Commercial Revolution** marked an important step in the transition of Europe. European rulers attempted to increase their wealth through **mercantilism** — the belief that wealth and power were based on possessing of gold and silver. In order to obtain more precious metals, European rulers established overseas colonies in the Americas, Asia, and Africa. In this same period, merchants and bankers laid the foundation for the system known as **capitalism**. Under capitalism, business owners risked their capital *(money)* in order to make profits. Joint stock companies, bankers, and merchants invested in overseas trade and lent money to European rulers.

THE RISE OF ROYAL POWER

The Renaissance, Protestant Reformation, and the decline of feudalism all led to an increase in the power of European monarchs. The Wars of Religion allowed them to build large standing armies and to collect more taxes. Kings justified their increased power on the basis of divine right. **Divine Right Theory** taught that the king was God's deputy on Earth, and that royal commands expressed God's wishes.

FRANCE UNDER LOUIS XIV

The Englishman **Thomas Hobbes** wrote that kings were justified in assuming absolute power because only they could maintain order in a society. This idea, along with divine right theory, helped give rise to **absolutism** — the holding of unlimited power. **Louis XIV** (1638-1715) of France was a model for other absolute rulers. To subdue the French nobles, Louis built a palace at **Versailles**, where he forced them to live under his watchful eye. His laws regulated industry and commerce, and he forced French Protestants to convert to Catholicism or leave France.

At Versailles, French nobles competed for the King's attention.

Jarrett Archives

RUSSIA UNDER THE TSARS

The Tsars of Russia adopted absolutism on a giant scale. Unlike Western Europe, serfdom had continued in Russia. **Peter the Great** (1682-1725) turned Russia from a backward nation into a modern power by forcefully introducing Western ideas, culture, and technology to Russia in a short period of time. Peter used brutal methods to force his nobles to adopt Western customs. He moved the capital of Russia from Moscow to St. Petersburg, a city he built on the Baltic Sea, so that Russia would have a "window on the West." **Catherine the Great** (1762-1796) continued Peter's policies of Westernization and the expansion of Russian territory.

BRITAIN BECOMES A LIMITED MONARCHY

Unlike other European rulers, the kings of Britain *(England, Scotland and Wales)* were never able to secure absolute power. In 1215, King John had been forced to sign a document called the **Magna Carta**, guaranteeing his nobles that they could not be fined or imprisoned except according to the law of the land. England later developed a powerful **Parliament**, a legislature composed of nobles and elected representatives. When Charles I attempted to rule Britain without Parliament, he was overthrown and beheaded in the **Puritan Revolution** (1642-1649). The monarchy was restored in 1660, but the **Glorious Revolution** (1688) substituted a new monarch and confirmed the supremacy of Parliament. The **Bill of Rights of 1689** stated that the king could not introduce new taxes or raise an army without Parliament's consent.

These events were justified by the writings of **John Locke**. Locke wrote that governments obtain their power from the people they govern, not from God. The main purpose of government, Locke believed, was to protect people's life, liberty, and property. People therefore had a right to rebel if government abused its power. A century later, his writings greatly influenced leaders of the American and French Revolutions.

THE SCIENTIFIC REVOLUTION

The Scientific Revolution began during the Renaissance and continued into the 18th century. It rejected traditional authority and church teachings in favor of the **scientific method** — in which scientists observed nature, made hypotheses, and tested their ideas through experiments. **Sir Isaac Newton** used the scientific method to develop the law of gravity — a single formula that explained the movement of all the planets and the speed of objects falling on Earth. His discovery raised hopes that the entire universe acted according to fixed laws, which scientists could discover.

THE ENLIGHTENMENT

The success of the Scientific Revolution and Europe's increasing wealth led to the Enlightenment in the 1700s. Enlightenment thinkers believed that by applying reason and science, they could better understand nature and human society. They questioned the divine right of kings, the privileges of the nobility, and the power of the Church.

KEY THINKERS OF THE ENLIGHTENMENT

- **Voltaire** (1694-1778) poked fun at traditional authority in society, government, and the church. His views on religious toleration and intellectual freedom greatly influenced the leaders of the American and French Revolutions.

- **Jean-Jacques Rousseau** (1712-1778) believed a government should express the "general will" of the people. His book *The Social Contract* helped to inspire the democratic ideals of the French Revolution.

- **Montesquieu** (1689-1755) argued for separation of powers in government as a check against tyranny. His book *The Spirit of Laws* later encouraged the development of a system of checks and balances in the U.S. Constitution.

- **Adam Smith** (1723-1790) described capitalism in his book *The Wealth of Nations*. Smith explained how competition and the division of labor help to guide a free-market economic system based on self-interest.

THE TERRITORIAL EMPIRES OF ASIA

While Europeans were creating a new global order in the West, large empires continued to flourish in Turkey, Persia, India, and China. These territorial Asian rulers used firearms and large standing armies to maintain their power. However, these empires did not advance as rapidly in science and technology as did European states in the same period, and they would later feel the impact of European expansion.

THE OTTOMAN EMPIRE

The **Ottoman Turks** emerged as rulers of the Islamic world in the 1200s. By 1453 they had captured Constantinople, the capital of what was left of the once-great Byzantine Empire. At the heart of the Ottoman system of government was the **Sultan** (*ruler*) and his court. The Ottomans accommodated the cultural diversity of their empire, however, and allowed Christian and Jewish communities largely to govern themselves.

THE SAFAVID EMPIRE

The **Safavids** created a Muslim empire in Persia *(present-day Iran)* in the 1500s. They excelled at miniature painting, carpet-making, literature, medicine, and astronomy. Warfare with the Ottomans weakened the Safavids; they were conquered in 1771.

MUSLIM, MUGHAL, AND BRITISH INDIA

In the 11th and 12th centuries, Muslim invaders established independent kingdoms, known as **Sultanates**, throughout northern India. In the 1500s the Mughal Empire emerged. The **Mughals** were Muslims with close ties to Safavid Persia. Their most fa-

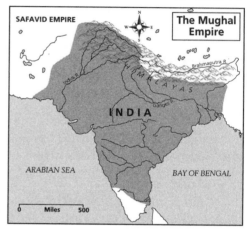

mous ruler, **Akbar the Great** (1542-1605) united northern India in a series of fierce campaigns, but later became tolerant towards Hindus, promoting peace and prosperity. His grandson, **Shah Jahan** (1628-1658) built the magnificent **Taj Mahal**, a tomb for his favorite wife. Jahan's successor, however, was hostile to Hindus, reimposing special taxes on them and destroying their temples. This set the stage for bloodshed beween Muslims and Hindus in India for centuries to come. Meanwhile, British and French merchants established trading posts along India's southern coasts. The **British East India Company** increased its power and influence through a series of alliances with local rulers. By the late 1700s, the British defeated their French rivals and were poised to take control of the Indian sub-continent.

THE MING AND QING DYNASTIES IN CHINA

After overthrowing the Mongols, China enjoyed nearly 300 years of peace under the **Ming Dynasty** (1368-1644). Chinese literature and art flourished. Trade in silks, porcelains, and other luxury goods prospered. China expanded to include Korea, Burma, and Vietnam. Eventually, however, corruption among public officials, population growth, and peasant uprisings weakened the Ming government. In 1644 the Manchus invaded China from the north and founded the **Qing (Manchu) Dynasty** (1644-1912). Like previous invaders, the Manchus adopted Chinese ways. They continued traditional civil service examinations and patronized Chinese literature, art, and music. By 1750, China had more than 150 million people and several large urban centers. Even so, European technology gradually surpassed that of China during these years.

SUMMARIZING YOUR UNDERSTANDING

OVERARCHING THEME

*Contacts among different cultures often lead to
the spread of new ideas and historical change.*

MAJOR IDEAS

CHANGE
- The encounter between Europe and the Americas was a major turning point in world history, leading to profound changes in Europe, America, Africa, and Asia.

CULTURE AND INTELLECTUAL LIFE
- European, Native American, and African traditions blended together to create Latin American values, ideals, and culture.

INTERDEPENDENCE
- The exchange of new products fostered by European exploration aand colonization welded together a truly world-wide economy for the first time.

GEOGRAPHY
- The location of the countries of Western Europe along the Atlantic gave them an advantage in overseas trade.

POLITICAL SYSTEMS
- The territorial empires of Eurasia — Ottoman, Persian, Mughal, and Ming/Qing — combined absolute rule with firearms and large standing armies.

IMPORTANT TERMS, CONCEPTS, AND PEOPLE

- ✦ Maya, Aztec, Inca
- ✦ Age of Discovery
- ✦ Hernando Cortés
- ✦ Francisco Pizarro
- ✦ Cultural Diffusion
- ✦ Transatlantic Slave Trade
- ✦ Age of Kings
- ✦ Peter the Great
- ✦ Mercantilism
- ✦ Divine Right Theory
- ✦ Absolutism
- ✦ Glorious Revolution
- ✦ John Locke
- ✦ Scientific Revolution
- ✦ Isaac Newton
- ✦ Enlightenment
- ✦ Voltaire
- ✦ Jean-Jacques Rousseau
- ✦ Montesquieu
- ✦ Adam Smith
- ✦ Ottoman Empire
- ✦ Akbar the Great
- ✦ Shah Jahan
- ✦ Qing (*Manchu*) Dynasty

TESTING YOUR UNDERSTANDING

1   One main reason European nations sought an all-water route to Asia was that
    1 they needed a place to send their excess populations
    2 Asia represented a place to sell manufactured goods
    3 the fall of the Byzantine Empire cut Europe off from trade with East Asia
    4 Muslims had gained control of the Holy Land

2   Which characteristic was common to both the ancient Egyptians and the Maya?
    1 monotheistic religion   3 the influence of European cultures
    2 nomadic lifestyles   4 written forms of communication

3   During the colonial period in Latin America, a major reason for the importation of
    Africans as slaves was the
    1 scarcity of Native American labor   3 development of advanced farming
    2 need for skilled industrial workers 4 desire to promote Christianity

4   Which was an immediate result of the European Age of Exploration?
    1 Islamic culture spread across Africa and Asia.
    2 European influence spread to the Western Hemisphere.
    3 Independence movements developed in Asia and Africa.
    4 Military dictatorships were established throughout Europe.

5   The concept of mercantilism is best illustrated by the
    1 political structure of China during the Zhou dynasty
    2 social kinship system of the Kushite people
    3 military strategies of the armies of the Roman Empire
    4 economic relationship between Spain and its Latin American colonies

6   In an outline, one of these is a main topic, and the other three are sub-topics.
    Which is the main topic?
    1 Signing of Magna Carta
    2 Development of Constitutional Monarchy
    3 Start of the Glorious Revolution
    4 Rise of Parliament

7   During the Age of Kings (1600s and 1700s), European monarchies
    1 sought to increase the civil rights of their citizens
    2 tried to centralize their political power
    3 attempted to develop better relations with Muslim rulers
    4 sought to encourage the growth of cooperative farms

8   Which was a result of the Commercial Revolution?
    1 decline in population growth in Europe
    2 shift of power from Western Europe to Eastern Europe
    3 spread of feudalism throughout Western Europe
    4 expansion of European influence overseas

9   The Ottoman, Safavid, and Mughal Empires were similar in that they all
    1 were followers of Islam   3 were located in Europe
    2 limited the power of their rulers   4 depended on their large navies

THEMATIC ESSAY QUESTION

Directions: Write a well-organized essay that includes an introduction, several paragraphs explaining your position, and a conclusion.

Theme: Movement of Goods and People

> Cultural diffusion often takes place when one society establishes contact with or conquers another society.

Task:

Choose *two* examples from your study of global history and geography in which one society established contact with or conquered another society.

For *each* example:
- Describe one way in which the two societies were changed.
- Explain how cultural diffusion resulted.

You may use any example from your study of global history and geography. Some suggestions you may wish to consider include: ancient Greece, ancient Rome, the Islamic Empire, the Crusades, the Mongols, and the Age of Discovery.

You are *not* limited to these suggestions.

CHAPTER 9

NEW CURRENTS: REVOLUTION, INDUSTRY, AND NATIONALISM, 1770 - 1900

A person from the Middle Ages would not have felt too out of place living in Renaissance Italy. Likewise, a person living in Japan during the Heian Period would not have felt uncomfortable there 300 years later. But this would *not* be true for someone who lived in France before the French Revolution and returned a century later. The pace of social and economic change increased dramatically in this period, altering lifestyles almost beyond recognition. In reviewing this era, it is easiest to group these changes into four areas:

CHANGES IN THE WORLD, MID-1700s TO 1900

- **The French Revolution** had a world-wide impact. It challenged the way people thought about traditional political authority and divisions in society.

- **The Industrial Revolution** caused the greatest changes in lifestyles since the dawn of civilization. New sources of power replaced human and animal power. People began to mass-produce goods with machines in factories.

- **Nationalism** created difficulties for countries with many nationalities under their control. National groups under foreign rule frequently attempted to acquire their own national states. Italy and Germany emerged as new states.

- **Imperialism** changd the map of the world. The new capabilities provided by the Industrial Revolution and the ambitions inspired by nationalism caused the leading European powers to claim vast areas of Asia, Africa, and the Pacific.

The impact of European imperialism caused the power of traditional empires like China to erode. The country most able to resist European domination by copying foreign ways turned out to be Japan. In studying this era, you should focus the following:

✦ What were the causes and effects of the French Revolution?
✦ What were the causes and effects of the Industrial Revolution?
✦ What factors led to an upsurge in nationalistic feeling in the 1800s?
✦ What were the benefits and drawbacks of imperialism in Africa and Asia?

THE FRENCH REVOLUTION AND ITS IMPACT

THE FRENCH REVOLUTION

On the eve of the revolution, France was the most populous and powerful country in Western Europe. French absolutism had provided a model for many other states.

PRECONDITIONS TO REVOLUTION

French society was divided into three classes, or "estates": the First Estate was the clergy, the Second Estate the nobles, and the Third Estate consisted of the commoners. The nobles had special privileges, such as being exempt from most taxes. Only nobles could fill certain posts in the army or the king's court. The largest group of commoners were peasants, but the most important group in the Third Estate were the **bourgeoisie** (*merchants, professionals, and shopkeepers*). The bourgeoisie grew to resent the special privileges of the nobility.

THE REVOLUTION BEGINS

In the 1700s, French kings had virtually bankrupted the state through costly wars and borrowing. By the late 1780s the ministers of **King Louis XVI** believed the only way to solve the government's financial problems was to tax the nobility. However, the nobles refused to pay taxes unless the king first summoned an **Estates General** — a national assembly representing all three estates. When the Estates General met in 1789, the focus quickly shifted to the bourgeoisie's grievances, and events took an unexpected turn. The Third Estate declared themselves to be a **National Assembly**. They issued the **Declaration of the Rights of Man**, abolished the privileges of the clergy and the nobles, and adopted a new constitution limiting the king's powers. People in Paris showed their support for the Assembly by storming the Bastille prison and freeing the prisoners. The revolution came to stand for democratic government and social equality. Its slogan was "Liberty, Equality, and Fraternity" (*brotherhood*).

THE REVOLUTION TAKES A RADICAL TURN

Other European rulers grew alarmed at the events unfolding in France. A war broke out, and radicals in France gained control of the new government. They executed King Louis XVI and turned France into a republic. The new **Committee of Public Safety** took charge of the revolution. Led by **Maximilien Robespierre**, the committee armed ordinary citizens and began a **Reign of Terror** to save France from foreign invasion. Thousands of suspected traitors were executed. These policies proved successful, but power shifted back to more moderate leaders after the threat of foreign invasion passed.

THE RISE AND FALL OF NAPOLEON

A young general, **Napoleon Bonaparte** (1769-1821), invaded Italy and defeated the Austrians and Russians. In 1799, Napoleon seized power in France and became a dictator. He introduced the **Civil Code** (codified law) and other reforms.

MILITARISM AND THE NAPOLEONIC EMPIRE

In 1804, Napoleon declared himself French Emperor. Within a year he defeated all the European powers except Britain. Napoleon combined the social reforms of the revolution with his own absolute power. However, his ambition united most of Europe against him. In 1812, Napoleon invaded Russia with 400,000 soldiers. Russians burned their crops and buildings rather than surrender. When Napoleon reached Moscow, the Russians had set the city on fire. In the bitter winter, Napoleon's army retreated. Only one in ten soldiers survived. In 1814, Britain, Russia, Prussia, and Austria united to invade France, and overthrew Napoleon.

THE CONGRESS OF VIENNA (1814-1815)

European leaders brought the French royal family back to the throne. Then they met at Vienna to redraw the map of Europe. The **Great Powers** (*Britain, Russia, Austria, and Prussia*) restored many former rulers and borders, but also redistributed territories to establish a more stable **"balance of power."** This gave each of the Great Powers enough military strength that no single power such as France could dominate the others.

THE BIRTH OF NATIONALISM

In redrawing the map of Europe, **Prince Metternich** of Austria and the other leaders at Vienna ignored the spirit of nationalism ignited by the French Revolution. **Nationalism** is the belief that each "nation" or ethnic group should have its own country and government. For thirty years after the Congress of Vienna, Europe experienced repeated revolutions caused by nationalism and economic unrest. In 1848, nationalist revolutions broke out across Europe, but were crushed by Austria, Prussia, and Russia.

THE INDEPENDENCE OF LATIN AMERICA

One of the most far-reaching effects of the French Revolution was the independence of Latin America. After 1814, Spain and Portugal tried to re-impose colonial rule. This attempt, combined with the ideals of the American and French Revolutions and the efforts of **Simon Bolivar**, triggered independence movements throughout Mexico and South America. After independence, many countries fell under the rule of powerful political bosses known as **caudillos**.

THE INDUSTRIAL REVOLUTION

The **Industrial Revolution** refers to a revolution in making things — using machines and new sources of power in factories, instead of making goods at home by hand. The Industrial Revolution began in Great Britain in the 1700s. Britain's island location, natural resources, powerful middle class, and colonial empire gave it many unique advantages. A series of inventions, including the spinning jenny, steam engine, and power loom, enabled British entrepreneurs to mass-produce goods in factories.

THE EMERGENCE OF INDUSTRIAL CAPITALISM

Large numbers of workers became employed in factories. A new middle class of factory-owners, merchants, and bankers emerged. As these capitalists grew richer, conditions for many of the working class worsened. Early factories were often unsafe. Men, women, and children worked long hours for low wages and faced periodic unemployment. The new capitalist class promoted the doctrine of **laissez-faire capitalism**, which rejected government interference between business-owners and their workers.

DEMANDS FOR REFORM

The social problems of the Industrial Revolution caused demands for reform. Workers joined unions and threatened to strike for better conditions. Eventually, laws limiting child and female labor and improving working conditions were passed in Britain and other countries. Two leading critics of early capitalism were **Karl Marx** (1818-1882) and **Friedrich Engels**. Their *Communist Manifesto* (1848) set forth the basic ideas of **Communism**. They believed that every society is divided into conflicting classes. In industrial societies, the capitalists owned the means of production and lived off the labor of the workers (*proletariat*). Marx and Engels predicted that eventually the proletariat would rise up in a violent revolution and overthrow the capitalists. Then the workers would establish a new Communist society in which factories and other valuable resources would be owned in common, and class struggle would end.

NATIONALISM AND IMPERIALISM

THE UNIFICATION OF ITALY AND GERMANY

For centuries, Italy and Germany had each been divided into many small states. Nationalists had sought to unify these states in the **Revolution of 1848**, but had failed.

ITALIAN UNIFICATION (1859-1870)

Count Cavour became the Prime Minister of Piedmont. With French help, he drove the Austrians out of northern Italy in the War of 1859. Cavour then annexed most of northern and central Italy. In the south, the nationalist leader **Giuseppi Garibaldi** overthrew the King of Naples. Garibaldi agreed to add Naples to Cavour's enlarged Piedmont to create the Kingdom of Italy in 1860.

GERMAN UNIFICATION (1863-1871)

Soon after Italian unification was achieved, **Otto Von Bismarck** was appointed Prime Minister of Prussia, the largest state in Northern Germany. Using a policy of "**blood and iron,**" Bismarck engaged in a rapid series of successful wars against Denmark, Austria, and France in order to unite Germany by 1871. The King of Prussia then became the **Kaiser** (*emperor*) of all of Germany.

REPRESSION IN RUSSIA

In Russia, the Tsars continued to hold absolute power as autocrats. After Russia was defeated by Britain and France in the **Crimean War** (1854-1856), Tsar **Alexander II** listened to reformers and emancipated the serfs in 1861. Later Tsars opposed change and used repression to maintain order. Influenced by nationalism, they adopted the policy of **Russification**, in which non-Russians in the empire were forced to adopt Russian culture and use the Russian language. Jews in Russia faced government-organized riots, known as **pogroms**, while the Tsar became the protector of Slavic people in the Balkans.

THE DECLINE OF OTTOMAN TURKEY

The forces of nationalism also helped accelerate the decline of the Ottoman Empire. Ottoman rulers had failed to keep pace with Western technology. As nationalism spread, the difficulties of governing the diverse peoples of the Ottoman Empire grew. In the late 1870s, rebellions in the Balkans and pressures from Russia led to the independence of several Slavic nations.

THE "NEW IMPERIALISM"

Imperialism refers to the political and economic control of one country by another. In the 1880s interest in imperialism suddenly revived when new European nations sought their own colonies. In addition, many Europeans believed in **Social Darwinism** — the idea (based on Charles Darwin's theory of the "survival of the fittest") that some societies were superior to others because they were more successful. Europeans now had rifles, steamships, trains, and new medicines, allowing them to go deep into the African interior. They also needed more raw materials and markets for their new industries.

THE BRITISH IN INDIA

British rule in India brought many advantages, such as the construction of railroads, schools, hospitals, and colleges. English became the main language of government. However, many Indians resented British rule and control. This discontent erupted during the **Sepoy Mutiny** of 1857. After crushing the rebellion, the British government took over formal rule of India from the British East India Company.

THE "SCRAMBLE FOR AFRICA"

In the 1880s, Europeans engaged in a "Scramble for Africa," in which most of Africa came under their direct control. European medicine, hospitals, and improved nutrition increased the life spans of many Africans. Europeans also introduced telegraph lines, railroads, and other modern technologies. However, most Africans were forced to work long hours in mines, on plantations, or as servants for their European masters. Europeans had no respect for local traditions and treated Africans as inferior. Their colonial boundaries ignored older tribal boundaries and divided Africans artificially. African resources were used mostly to benefit Europeans, not Africans.

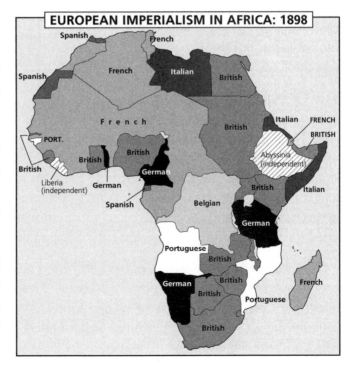

EUROPEAN IMPERIALISM IN AFRICA: 1898

EUROPEAN "SPHERES OF INFLUENCE" IN CHINA

Even China now felt the effects of European imperialism. Western nations were interested in China because of its huge population, which offered a giant market for European manufactured goods. The British defeated the Chinese in the **Opium War** (1839-42), and forced China to open several ports in which the British were given exclusive trading privileges. Other European countries demanded similar **"spheres of influence."** The United States, to preserve its own trading rights, declared the **Open Door Policy** in 1899. This policy discouraged European powers from further dividing up China, and helped keep China "open" to trade. Many Chinese resented the growing foreign influence in their homeland. That same year, a Chinese group known as the "Boxers" arose in rebellion and attacked foreign residents in China. The Boxers were secretly supported by the imperial government, but an international expeditionary force intervened and crushed the **Boxer Rebellion**.

THE OPENING OF JAPAN
AND THE MEIJI RESTORATION

The **Tokugawa Shogunate** banned foreigners and isolated Japan from foreign influences. In 1853, the United States sent a naval squadron under **Commodore Matthew Perry** to Japan, to open the country to American trade. Knowing what had happened to China in the Opium War, Japanese leaders were fearful, and reopened Japan to foreign trade. The Shogun was severely criticized for this, and fifteen years later the Shogunate collapsed.

Emperor Meiji, whose ancestors had been mere puppets for over a thousand years, was suddenly "restored" to power. Emperor Meiji was convinced that Japan had to adopt Western ways if it was to escape future domination by Western powers. Under his rule, Japan successfully imitated and adapted Western ways. Feudalism was abolished and the samurai lost their special social status. Within a few short years, Japan developed modern industries, improved education, and expanded its army and navy.

SUMMARIZING YOUR UNDERSTANDING

OVERARCHING THEME

*Historical turning points are decisions or events
that alter the direction history takes.*

MAJOR IDEAS

POLITICAL SYSTEMS
- The American and French Revolutions led to new views of political authority, challenging the power of absolute rulers.

NATIONALISM
- Nationalism has been both a unifying and a divisive force in history.

SCIENCE AND TECHNOLOGY
- Industrialization is a powerful force capable of totally transforming a society.
- Technological superiority can allow one society to dominate another.

IMPERIALISM
- European imperialism had a mixed legacy for the peoples of Africa and Asia — introducing new ideas and technologies, at the cost of devaluing native cultures and seizing local resources.

IMPORTANT TERMS, CONCEPTS, AND PEOPLE

- ✦ French Revolution
- ✦ Declar. of the Rights of Man
- ✦ Reign of Terror
- ✦ Robespierre
- ✦ Napoleon
- ✦ Congress of Vienna
- ✦ Metternich
- ✦ Balance of Power
- ✦ Industrial Revolution

- ✦ Laissez-faire capitalism
- ✦ Karl Marx
- ✦ *Communist Manifesto*
- ✦ Revolutions of 1848
- ✦ Russification
- ✦ Pogroms
- ✦ Count Cavour
- ✦ Guiseppi Garibaldi
- ✦ Otto von Bismarck

- ✦ New Imperialism
- ✦ Charles Darwin
- ✦ Sepoy Mutiny
- ✦ Spheres of Influence
- ✦ Opium War
- ✦ Open Door Policy
- ✦ Boxer Rebellion
- ✦ Matthew Perry
- ✦ Meiji Restoration

TESTING YOUR UNDERSTANDING

1   One important result of the French Revolution was that
1   France enjoyed a lengthy period of peace and prosperity
2   the Church was restored to its former role and power in France
3   political power shifted to the bourgeoisie
4   France lost its spirit of nationalism

Base your answer to question 2 on the graphs and on your knowledge of global history.

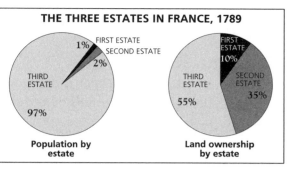

THE THREE ESTATES IN FRANCE, 1789

FIRST ESTATE 1%
SECOND ESTATE 2%
THIRD ESTATE 97%
Population by estate

FIRST ESTATE 10%
SECOND ESTATE 35%
THIRD ESTATE 55%
Land ownership by estate

2   Based on the graphs, which statement is most accurate?
1   The three estates in France owned land equally.
2   The second estate was the most numerous of the three.
3   The first two estates had landholdings out of proportion to their population size.
4   The total population of the first and second estates was larger than the third estate.

3   The main purpose of the Congress of Vienna (1814-1815) was to
1   restore a stable balance of power in Europe after the Napoleonic Wars
2   create a European Court of Justice
2   promote the ideas of the French Revolution
4   preserve the Ottoman Empire

4   Which quotation best reflects a feeling of nationalism?
1   "An eye for an eye and a tooth for a tooth."
2   "Do unto others as you would have others do unto you."
3   "For God, King, and Country."
4   "Opposition to evil is as much a duty as is cooperation with good."

5   The invention of spinning and weaving machinery increased the number of workers in the textile industry in Europe because
1   early textile machinery could not produce goods as efficiently as hand labor
2   laws prohibited women and children from working with machinery
3   the demand for textiles increased as they became cheaper to produce
4   unions required that more workers be hired to maintain the machines

6   Both the Sepoy Mutiny in India and the Boxer Rebellion in China attempted to
   1 end foreign domination   3 promote imperialism
   2 halt the trading of illegal drugs   4 overthrow Mongol rule

7   "All great nations ... have desired to set their mark upon barbarian lands, and those
who fail to participate in this great quest will play a pitiable role in times to come."
This quotation supports the concept of
   1 socialism   3 revolution
   2 human rights   4 imperialism

8   During the 19th century, the African continent was affected most by
   1 the Commercial Revolution   3 the Crusades
   2 the introduction of socialism   4 European imperialism

9   Peter the Great and the Meiji Emperor of Japan were similar in that both
   1 established democratic governments   3 converted to Christianity
   2 brought Western ideas to their nation   4 expanded political rights

THEMATIC ESSAY QUESTION

Directions: Write a well-organized essay that includes an introduction, several paragraphs explaining your position, and a conclusion.

Theme: Change

> Some events in global history are called "turning points" because
> they have had a significant political, social, or cultural impact.

Task:

> Choose *two* major turning points from your study of global history and geography.
>
> For *each* turning point:
> * Describe the event.
> * Explain the political, social, or cultural impact of that turning point in history.

You may use any example from your study of global history and geography. Some suggestions you may wish to consider include: Neolithic Revolution, Muslim conquests, Industrial Revolution, rise of West African Kingdoms, encounter between Europe and the Americas, French Revolution, Meiji Restoration.

You are *not* limited to these suggestions.

DOCUMENT-BASED ESSAY QUESTION

This task is based on the accompanying documents (1-6). Some of these documents have been edited for the purposes of this task. This task is designed to test your ability to work with historical documents. As you analyze the documents, take into account both the source of each document and the author's point of view.

Directions: Read the documents in Part A and answer the question after each document. Then read the directions for Part B and write your essay.

Historical Context:
Throughout history, societies have met the economic needs of their members in a variety of ways.

Task:
Compare and contrast some ways that societies have met the economic needs of their members. Evaluate the advantages and disadvantages of the way in which one of the societies discussed in the documents met those needs.

Part A
Short Answer

Directions: Analyze the documents and answer the questions that follow each document.

Document 1:

"The rich, getting possession of the greater part of undistributed lands, and being emboldened by the lapse of time to ... add to their holdings the small farms of their poor neighbors, partly by purchase and partly by force, came to cultivate vast tracts instead of single estates, using for this purpose slaves as laborers. Thus the powerful ones became enormously rich and the race of slaves multiplied throughout the country, while the Italian people dwindled in numbers and strength, being oppressed by poverty, taxes, and military service."

— Appian of Alexandria, a Roman historian,
discussing slavery in ancient Rome

1. What impact did the use of slaves have on ancient Roman society?

Document 2:

> "I work very hard. I go out at dawn, driving the oxen to the field, and I yoke them to the plough. However hard the winter, I dare not stay home for fear of my master. Having yoked the oxen and made the ploughshare fast to the plough, I have to plough a whole acre or more every day."
>
> — A serf's account of his typical day, recorded by an English monk (circa 1000 A.D.)

2. What role did serfs play in meeting the economic needs of medieval society? _____

Document 3:

> "The caliph (*ruler*) takes care of the poor, widows and orphans; pays them special pensions ... does the same for the blind. And, provided this does not overburden the treasury, builds hospitals for sick Muslims, with physicians and attendants who will cure them and minister to their needs ... The caliph distributes taxes then among all taxpayers in a fair, just and equitable manner; not exempting anyone because of his noble rank or great riches. He does not levy a tax on anyone which is beyond his capacity to pay."
>
> — Provincial Muslim governor Tahir Ibn al Hussein (775-822), describing the government's economic responsibilities

3. How were the less fortunate cared for in 8th and 9th century Muslim society? _____

Document 4:

> "When we arrived at the great square we were struck by the throngs of people and the amount of merchandise displayed. The chiefs who accompanied us showed us how the merchandise was kept separate. Let's start with the dealers in gold, silver and precious stones, feathers, cloth and embroidered goods, and other merchandise in the form of men and women to be sold as slaves. The slaves were tied to poles with collars around their necks so they couldn't escape. There were merchants who sold homespun clothing, cotton and thread, and others who sold cocoa ... There were people who sold henequen cloth, as well as rope and shoes made from the same plant. In another location they had skins of tigers, lions, deer and other animals, some tanned and others not."
>
> — A conquistador reveals an aspect of Aztec life

4. How did this market help to meet the economic needs of the Aztecs? _____

Document 5:

The photograph at right was taken in England in the 1800s.

5. What does this photograph tell us about 19-century England?

_____

_____

_____

Library of Congress

Document 6:

MAJOR INVENTIONS OF THE INDUSTRIAL REVOLUTION

Invention	Inventor	Date	Invention	Inventor	Date
Spinning jenny	James Hargreaves	1764	Power loom	Edmund Cartwright	1785
Water frame	Richard Arkwright	1769	Cotton gin	Eli Whitney	1793
Steam engine	James Watt	1769	Steamboat	Robert Fulton	1807
Spinning mule	Samuel Crompton	1779	Telegraph	Samuel Morse	1837

6. Explain how one of these inventions helped meet people's economic needs. _____

_____

Part B — Essay

Directions:
- Write a well-organized essay that includes an introduction, several paragraphs, and a conclusion.
- Use evidence from the documents to support your response.
- Do not simply repeat the contents of the documents.
- Include specific related information.

Task:

Using information from the documents and your knowledge of global history, write an essay in which you:
- Compare and contrast some ways in which societies have met the economic needs of their members.
- Evaluate the advantages and disadvantages of the way in which one of the societies discussed in the documents met those needs.

CHAPTER 10

THE WORLD AT WAR
1900 - 1945

In this era, industrialization and nationalism led to the rise of new political systems like Communism and Fascism. Humankind experienced the two most devastating wars in history. European world domination ended as the U.S. and the Soviet Union emerged as superpowers. It is helpful to divide this complex era into four main stages:

FOUR KEY STAGES FROM 1900
THROUGH THE TWO WORLD WARS

- **Pre-War Years (1900-1914):** As the century began, educated elites, frustrated by their nations' problems, often sought change through revolution. Meanwhile, European countries armed themselves for war. In Asia and Africa, European powers controlled vast colonial empires.

- **World War I (1914-1918):** A crisis between Austria-Hungary and Serbia led to war in Europe. In 1917, a Communist revolution took Russia out of the war. After the war, imperial governments in Austria-Hungary, Germany, and Turkey ended. New states arose in Eastern Europe.

- **The Inter-War Years (1919-1939):** The late 1920s saw general prosperity, followed by the world-wide Great Depression of the 1930s. Economic crisis gave rise to Fascist dictators such as Hitler in Germany and Mussolini in Italy. Meanwhile, Stalin ruled over the Communist Soviet Union with an iron fist.

- **World War II (1939-1945):** German and Japanese aggression plunged the world into war. The war resulted in the dropping of the atomic bomb, the birth of the United Nations, and the end of imperialism in Africa and Asia. The United States and Soviet Union emerged as global superpowers.

In studying this era, you should focus on the following questions:

✦ What conditions led to revolutionary changes in Turkey, Mexico, China, and Russia in the early 20th century?

✦ What changes did Lenin and Stalin introduce to the Soviet Union?

✦ What factors led to the rise of Fascism in Europe and militarism in Japan?

✦ What were the main causes and effects of both World War I and II?

THE CRISIS OF THE EARLY 20ᵀᴴ CENTURY

In the early years of the twentieth century, nationalist reformers in Russia, Turkey, Mexico, and China sought to overthrow their existing governments.

Russia. Revolts broke out throughout the country after Russia lost the **Russo-Japanese War** (1904-05). **Tsar Nicholas II** was forced to grant limited reforms.

Turkey. The Sultan was overthrown in 1908 by a group known as **Young Turks**. They encouraged industrialization, public education, and better treatment of women.

— REFORM THROUGH REVOLUTION —

Mexico. Dictator Porfirio Diaz was overthrown, and the **Mexican Revolution of 1910** began. After a civil war, the government introduced the **Constitution of 1917**, establishing public education, universal voting, an 8-hour workday, and the right to strike.

China. Uprisings in 1911 forced the Manchu Emperor to abdicate his throne. China became a republic. **Sun Yat-Sen** became head of the new government in 1916. He introduced three principles: Democracy, Nationalism and the Peoples' Livelihood.

THE OUTBREAK OF WORLD WAR I

By 1914, nationalism and other factors brought all of Europe into World War I. The underlying causes of the war included:

❖ **Nationalism.** Nationalistic feeling encouraged rivalries between the leading nations of Europe. It also led to new demands by ethnic minorities in Austria-Hungary, threatening to tear apart the Austro-Hungarian Empire.

❖ **Economic Rivalries and Imperialism.** Competition for economic supremacy and overseas colonies created further tension among the major powers.

❖ **The Alliance System.** Europe was divided into two alliances. On one side were Germany and Austria-Hungary. On the other were Britain, France, and Russia. An attack on one alliance member was considered an attack on the whole alliance.

❖ **Militarism.** Europeans were arming for war, which many saw as inevitable. The buildup of weapons and armies emboldened military leaders, who believed it would be better to attack than to wait to be attacked.

THE WAR BEGINS

In 1914, **Archduke Francis Ferdinand** of Austria-Hungary was assassinated by Slav nationalists. Austrians rightly believed Serb officials had helped the assassins, and invaded Serbia. The incident set off a chain reaction: Russia intervened to protect Serbia, and Germany to protect Austria-Hungary; Britain and France then entered because of their alliance commitments. In a matter of weeks, all of Europe was at war.

THE CONDUCT OF THE WAR

World War I brought a new and deadly form of warfare that the world had never seen before. New weapons such as machine guns, poison gas, submarines, and airplanes made it difficult to advance. Across Europe, soldiers dug trenches protected by barbed wire and machine guns. The United States was officially neutral, but when German submarines attacked American ships bringing supplies to Britain and France, the United States entered the war in 1917. The U.S. entry into the war broke the deadlock in Europe. In 1918, Germany and Austria-Hungary, weary of war, surrendered.

THE PEACE SETTLEMENT

U.S. President **Woodrow Wilson** announced America's plan for peace in the **Fourteen Points**. These promised to redraw the map of Europe to give each major nationality its own country. The Fourteen Points also promised freedom of the seas, an end to secret diplomacy, and the creation of the League of Nations. Believing that Wilson's offer would be the basis of the peace settlement, the Germans agreed to end the war. But the **Treaty of Versailles** (1919) was harsher than Germans had expected.

RESULTS OF WORLD WAR I

- **German Territorial Losses**. Germany lost territory to France and Poland, as well as all its overseas colonies.

- **Punishing Germany**. Germany lost its navy. Its army was reduced to a small police force. Germany was forced to accept blame for starting the war and to pay huge **reparations** *(payment for damages)* to the Allies.

- **Austria-Hungary and Turkey**. The Austro-Hungarian Empire was divided up into several smaller states such as Czechoslovakia and Yugoslavia. Turkey lost most of its territories in the Middle East. **Kemal Atatürk** led a revolt that overthrew the Sultanate and created a new Turkish republic.

- **League of Nations**. The Treaty of Versailles created a League of Nations. Members agreed to defend each other against aggressors. However, several major powers, such as the United States and Russia, refused to join.

THE RUSSIAN REVOLUTION OF 1917

Another major consequence of World War I was the Russian Revolution. Military disasters in World War I led to widespread desertion in the Russian army. Fighting also cut railroad lines, preventing food from reaching Russian cities. In March 1917, when soldiers refused to fire on striking workers, Tsar Nicholas II gave up his throne. The leaders of a new provisional government declared Russia a republic. Soon Communist revolutionaries known as **Bolsheviks**, led by **Vladimir Lenin**, called for the overthrow of the new government and withdrawal from the war. The Bolsheviks promised the Russian people **"Peace, Bread, and Land."** The Bolsheviks seized power in a second revolution in November 1917. A brutal civil war followed, which the Bolsheviks won. Once in power, the Bolsheviks renamed themselves "Communists" and changed the name of Russia to the Union of Soviet Socialist Republics (USSR) or **Soviet Union**.

THE WORLD BETWEEN THE WARS: PROSPERITY AND DEPRESSION

The first years after the war were not easy ones, especially in the new Soviet Union, where Communists leaders introduced profound changes with a long-lasting impact.

THE SOVIET UNION UNDER LENIN AND STALIN

Under Lenin, all industries in the Soviet Union were nationalized. Lands were transferred to the peasants. Lenin briefly allowed limited private ownership in his **New Economic Policy** (N.E.P.) When Lenin died in 1924, **Joseph Stalin** took power by outmaneuvering his rivals. Stalin established a totalitarian state in which all aspects of public and private life were controlled. Free speech and dissent were forbidden. The secret police arrested suspected opponents, who were sent to **gulags** (*prison labor camps*) in Siberia. Stalin seized peasant lands to create state-managed **collective farms**. Stalin then sought to turn the Soviet Union into a modern industrial state through a series of **Five Year Plans**, setting national goals and controlling all aspects of the economy.

PROSPERITY AND THEN DEPRESSION

The human and material costs of World War I were staggering. People in many parts of the world suffered famine and malnutrition. Europeans spent the first years after the war rebuilding and recovering. Meanwhile, the United States emerged from the war as the world's greatest economic power. Prosperity in America gradually spread to Europe and the rest of the world. New values emerged, and women gained the right to vote in the U.S., Great Britain and other countries. But in 1929, the economic

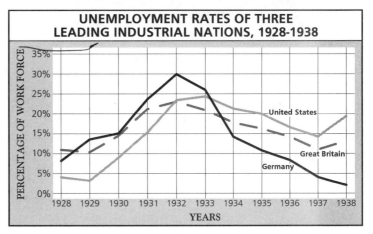

bubble burst when the **New York Stock Market** crashed. The U.S. economy fell into a **depression** — a severe economic downturn marked by high unemployment, falling prices, and low production. International trade declined drastically, American bankers called in loans made to Europe, and the **Great Depression** spread worldwide.

THE RISE OF FASCISM

Fascism was a new political movement that appeared in Europe in the unsettled conditions after World War I. The term "Fascism" is taken from the name of the political party formed by **Benito Mussolini** in Italy, but is often used by historians to identify similar systems such as Nazism in Germany.

Fascists were extreme nationalists. They believed all social classes should unite into a single national party, following the will of an all-powerful leader. Fascists were opposed to such ideas as democracy, labor unions, and strikes. Instead, they were prepared to use violence and war to achieve their goals. Some long-held European beliefs helped prepare the way for Fascism, including racism and **anti-Semitism** *(hatred of Jews)*. Fascists were also Social Darwinists who applied Darwin's theory of evolution to human society. They believed all groups competed for survival, and that stronger groups had a right to rule weaker groups. Fascists felt they were superior and should dominate others. Mussolini became the first Fascist leader to seize power when he took control of Italy in 1922.

Two of Europe's most powerful Fascist dictators, Benito Mussolini (left) and Adolf Hitler

National Archives

THE WEIMAR REPUBLIC FAILS IN GERMANY

The German Kaiser abdicated at the end of the war. A democratic government known as the **Weimar Republic** replaced the monarchy. The Weimar Republic was severely criticized for signing the Treaty of Versailles and for being forced to pay huge reparations to Britain and France. Moreover, many Germans despised democratic ideals.

GERMANY UNDER NAZI CONTROL

The **Nazi Party**, led by **Adolf Hitler**, blamed Weimar leaders for Germany's troubles. Hitler believed Germans were a superior race who should rule the world. His book, *Mein Kampf*, called for Germans to repudiate the Versailles Treaty, eliminate Jews, seize lands to the east, and enslave neighboring peoples. When six million Germans lost their jobs during the Great Depression, popular support for the Nazis rose. In 1933, Hitler was appointed chief minister. Once in power, he outlawed all opposition and turned Germany into a totalitarian state. Opponents were arrested and executed without trial or sent to concentration camps. Jews were forced into ghettoes and millions were eventually murdered in concentration camps. Hitler rebuilt Germany's army and navy, and began many public works projects, returning Germany to full employment.

WORLD WAR II AND ITS AFTERMATH

The rise of Fascist dictators in Italy, Germany, and elsewhere made a new war almost inevitable. However, the war was postponed for several years while the dictators built up their armaments. Meanwhile, Japan had launched a war in East Asia in 1931.

THE ROAD TO WAR

The League of Nations Fails. The League relied on **collective security** to prevent another war. Hitler, in violation of the Treaty of Versailles, rebuilt his armed forces. The League could do nothing about it because its members refused to take action against dictators that might lead to war.

Failure of Appeasement. Hitler next claimed territories where Germans lived. He took Austria in 1938. Then British Prime Minister **Neville Chamberlain** met with Hitler in Munich and tried **appeasement** *(granting concessions to avoid war)*. Chamberlain agreed to Hitler's demand for the Sudetenland in western Czechoslovakia.

Invasion of Poland. In 1939, Hitler made a new demand for part of Poland. This time, Britain and France refused to give in. Hitler made a secret deal with Stalin to keep the Soviet Union out of the war. Germany then invaded Poland, starting World War II.

THE WAR AND ITS AFTERMATH

The German army quickly overran Poland, Holland, Belgium, Denmark, Norway and France. Only Britain held out by the end of 1940. In 1941, Hitler launched a surprise attack on the Soviet Union. By 1943, the Soviets began to push the Germans back.

THE WAR IN ASIA

The Japanese took advantage of the war in Europe to invade European colonies in Asia, including Singapore, Burma, Indonesia, and Indochina. However, the United States threatened a naval blockade. In response, Japan launched a surprise attack on **Pearl Harbor** in December, 1941, bringing the United States into the war.

THE TIDE TURNS

As Japan's ally, Germany also declared war on America. Allied leaders focused on defeating Germany first. In June 1944, Allied troops invaded France, as Soviet forces pushed in from the east. By May 1945, Germany surrendered. The U.S. now turned its full force to defeating Japan. In August 1945, the **Atomic Age** began when atomic bombs were dropped on **Hiroshima** and **Nagasaki**. Japan quickly surrendered.

THE HOLOCAUST

The **Holocaust** refers to the **genocide** *(murder of an entire people)* of Jews and others during World War II. Hitler built large concentration camps at Auschwitz and other places. People were transported to these camps from all over Nazi-controlled Europe to be murdered. The Nazis killed six million Jews, (two-thirds of all Jews then living in Europe), as well as many gypsies, Slavs, political prisoners, and people with disabilities.

THE NUREMBERG TRIALS

Nazi leaders were convicted by a tribunal at Nuremberg for "crimes against humanity." The trials revealed such atrocities as slave labor and medical experiments on humans.

THE ALLIED OCCUPATION OF GERMANY AND JAPAN

After the war, Germany was divided into four occupation zones, each of which was occupied by one of the Allied powers. Japan was occupied by U.S. forces. **General Douglas MacArthur** was given the task of reforming and rebuilding Japan.

Territorial Losses. Japan's overseas empire was taken away, leaving Japan with just her home islands.	**Leaders Punished**. Leaders responsible for wartime atrocities were put on trial and punished. Some 200,000 military, government, and business leaders were banned from holding government positions.

— CHANGES IMPOSED ON JAPAN —

Demilitarized. Japan's ability to wage war was virtually eliminated. Japan was forbidden to have an army or navy, except for a small "self-defense force." Japan also renounced the use of nuclear weapons.	**Constitution**. The Constitution of 1947 renounced war and made Japan a democratic nation. The emperor's political power was given to the people, but he remained their symbolic head of state.

THE BIRTH OF THE UNITED NATIONS

The victors formed a new peacekeeping organization, the **United Nations** (U.N.), as World War II ended. Major world powers were made members of the U.N. **Security Council**, where each member has veto power over peacekeeping and other operations.

ASIAN AND AFRICAN DECOLONIZATION

The war stimulated the demand for national self-determination in Africa and Asia. Over the next fifteen years, a dramatic transformation occurred throughout much of the world as former colonies became independent nations.

INDIA AND PAKISTAN

British India was the first major country to gain independence after the war. **Mohandas Gandhi**, leader of India's independence movement, used non-violent resistance, in which oppressors would gradually realize the futility of oppression. In 1930, Gandhi led a **"Salt March"** to protest the British salt tax. He also encouraged Indians to boycott the purchase of British goods. In 1947, the British government granted India its independence. To prevent violence between Hindus and Muslims, India was partitioned into India and Pakistan. Millions of Muslims and Hindus moved their homes, and large numbers of people were killed in the rioting that accompanied these migrations.

SOUTHEAST ASIA

Beginning in the 1500s, most of Southeast Asia had fallen under colonial rule. Japan occupied the region during World War II. After the war, the colonial powers attempted to regain control. In many areas, local nationalists demanded and achieved independence. In the Philippines (1946), Burma (1948) and Malaysia (1948), independence was achieved peacefully. The nations of Indonesia and Indochina (*now Cambodia, Laos, Vietnam*) achieved independence after years of bitter fighting,

THE MIDDLE EAST AND NORTH AFRICA

The French granted independence to Morocco, Tunisia, Libya, Lebanon, and Syria, and, after eight years of civil war, to Algeria. The British gave Saudi Arabia and Egypt independence even before the war, although Egypt remained a British satellite until its king was overthrown in the 1950s. The British finally withdrew from Palestine in 1947 and handed its future over to the United Nations, which voted to create Israel in 1948.

SUB-SAHARAN AFRICA

Many sub-Saharan colonies demanded independence after the war. **Kwame Nkrumah**, in the British colony called the Gold Coast, used Gandhi's method of peaceful protests and boycotts. His country won independence in 1957, and changed its name to Ghana. Other African leaders, including **Jomo Kenyatta** in Kenya and **Julius Nyerere** in Tanzania, followed Nkrumah's example. Over the next decade, almost all of sub-Saharan Africa achieved independence.

SUMMARIZING YOUR UNDERSTANDING

OVERARCHING THEME

The actions of some individuals have had a major impact on both their own societies and global history.

MAJOR IDEAS

GEOGRAPHY
- When powerful nations are located close to each other, their rivalries can lead to frequent conflicts.

CHANGE
- The two world wars led to profound changes in many nations.

POLITICAL SYSTEMS
- Communism and Fascism were two political systems based on using totalitarian rule to solve modern problems.

NATIONALISM
- Excessive national zeal made the 20th century the most destructive in history.
- Nationalism in Asia and Africa led to the end of European imperialism there.

SCIENCE AND TECHNOLOGY
- Improvements in technology have made warfare increasingly destructive.

JUSTICE AND HUMAN RIGHTS
- The crime of genocide can cross many cultures and time periods.

IMPORTANT TERMS, CONCEPTS, AND PEOPLE

- ✦ Mexican Revolution
- ✦ Sun Yat-Sen
- ✦ Young Turks
- ✦ Kemal Atatürk
- ✦ Alliance System
- ✦ Fourteen Points
- ✦ Treaty of Versailles
- ✦ Tsar Nicholas II
- ✦ "Peace, Bread, and Land"
- ✦ Vladimir Lenin
- ✦ Joseph Stalin
- ✦ Five-Year Plans
- ✦ Weimar Republic
- ✦ Fascism
- ✦ Adolf Hitler
- ✦ *Mein Kampf*
- ✦ Nazi Party
- ✦ Holocaust
- ✦ Hiroshima and Nagasaki
- ✦ Genocide
- ✦ Nuremberg Trials
- ✦ United Nations
- ✦ Mohandas Gandhi
- ✦ Salt March
- ✦ Decolonization
- ✦ Kwame Nkrumah
- ✦ Jomo Kenyatta

TESTING YOUR UNDERSTANDING

1 The harsh conditions imposed by the Treaty of Versailles after World War I helped lay the foundation for the
   1 rise of Nazism in Germany   3 fall of Porfiro Diaz in Mexico
   2 French Revolution   4 Bolshevik Revolution in Russia

2 Which provision of the Treaty of Versailles showed the intent of the Allies to punish the Central Powers for their role in World War I?
   1 "All nations shall maintain open convenants of peace."
   2 "Freedom of the seas will be maintained."
   3 "Germany will accept full responsibility for causing the war."
   4 "Territorial settlements shall be based on nationality."

Base your answer to question 3 on the line graph at right, and on your knowledge of global history.

GERMAN UNEMPLOYMENT, 1928-1933

3 Which statement is most accurate, based on the graph?
   1 German unemployment was highest in 1932.
   2 Between 1928 and 1933 German unemployment remained unchanged.
   3 By 1933, there were about 6 million unemployed German workers.
   4 The Nazi Party brought German unemployment under control in 1928.

4 Fascism in Europe during the 1920s and 1930s may best be described as a
   1 demonstration of laissez-faire capitalism that promoted free enterprise
   2 form of totalitarianism that glorified the nation above the individual
   3 type of economic system that stressed a classless society
   4 set of humanist ideals that emphasized an individual's worth and dignity

5 One similarity between Fascism and Communism, as practiced in the 1930s, was that both systems generally
   1 provided for hereditary rulers   3 supported democratic elections
   2 promoted ethnic diversity   4 suppressed opposition views

6 Which factor contributed most to the rise of totalitarian governments in Europe before World War II?

  1 improved educational systems   3 increasing political stability

  2 expanding democratic reforms   4 worsening economic conditions

Base your answer to question 7 on the bar graph and on your knowledge of global history.

7 According to the graph, which statement is most accurate?

  1 The costs of World War I were evenly spread among the warring nations.

  2 Russia spent more than any other nation.

  3 Germany spent more than Austria-Hungary, Italy, and Russia combined.

  4 Military costs were greatest at the start of World War I.

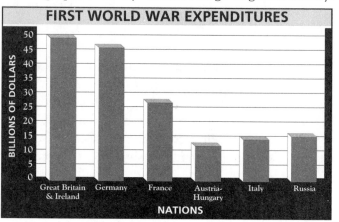

8 The French Revolution of 1789, the Chinese Revolution of 1911-1912, and the Russian Revolution of 1917 were similar in that all three revolutions

  1 were led by ruthless dictators   3 established a Communist state

  2 overthrew a monarch   4 led to prosperity for the middle classes

9 Stalin's Five-Year Plans and decision to form collective farms were examples of

  1 strategies to modernize the Soviet economy through forced Communism

  2 a more friendly foreign policy toward China

  3 methods of dealing with the United States during World War II

  4 programs to Westernize, educate, and enlighten the population

10 Which event was used by Mohandas Gandhi to bring world attention to the injustices of British colonialism in India?

  1 Salt March   3 Sepoy Mutiny

  2 outbreak of World War I   4 formation of India's Parliament

11 During India's independence movement, Mohandas Gandhi's boycott of British-made goods was effective because the British considered India a major

  1 shipping center   3 market for manufactured goods

  2 industrial center   4 source of mineral resources

12 Which statement about India is a fact rather than an opinion?
   1 Most Indians are happy with the practice of arranged marriages.
   2 India is fortunate to be country with religious diversity.
   3 The Mughals ruled India for more than 300 years.
   4 The partition of British India in 1947 helped India prosper.

13 Europeans dominated much of South and Southeast Asia in the 1800s mainly because
   1 Christianity appealed to the peoples of the region
   2 Europeans had more advanced technology
   3 the region lacked political organization
   4 few natural resources were found in the region

14 In 1947, the Indian subcontinent became independent and was divided into India and Pakistan. This division recognized the
   1 hostility between religious groups   3 natural geographic boundaries
   2 strength of Fascism   4 existing tribal divisions

THEMATIC ESSAY QUESTION

Directions: Write a well-organized essay that includes an introduction, several paragraphs explaining your position, and a conclusion.

Theme: Change

> The ideas and actions of some individuals have had a significant impact on others.

Task:

> Choose *two* individuals from your study of global history and geography.
>
> For *each* individual:
> • Explain how that individual's ideas or actions changed his or her own nation or another area of the world.
> • Explain one way in which the two individuals were similar or different.

You may use any example from your study of global history and geography. Some suggestions you may wish to consider include: Alexander the Great, Simon Bolivar, Martin Luther, Catherine the Great, Mohandas Gandhi, Adolf Hitler, Joseph Stalin, and Kwame Nkrumah.

You are *not* limited to these suggestions.

CHAPTER 11

FROM THE COLD WAR TO GLOBAL INTERDEPENDENCE, 1945 - PRESENT

At the end of World War II, two superpowers emerged: the United States and the Soviet Union. Their rivalry unleashed a "Cold War" that affected nearly every country on earth. Against this background of superpower rivalry, Western Europe and Japan recovered from the destruction of World War II to become economically powerful; developing nations struggled to improve their economies; and ethnic rivalries have turned many areas into global "hot spots." The collapse of Communism in the Soviet Union and Eastern Europe from 1989 to 1991 has led to equally monumental changes, in the final decade of the twentieth century.

KEY DEVELOPMENTS IN THE POSTWAR WORLD

- **The Cold War.** The Cold War started almost as soon as World War II ended. Eastern Europe, North Korea, and China quickly became Communist. From 1946 to the late 1980s, the U.S. and Soviet Union avoided a head-on confrontation. Instead, they engaged in a world-wide competition for influence, as well as regional conflicts such as the Vietnam War.

- **Problems of the Developing World.** While the superpowers engaged in the Cold War, the nations of Latin America, Africa, and Asia struggled to overcome poverty, illiteracy, ethnic conflicts, and political instability.

- **The Post-Cold War World.** Between 1989 and 1991, Communism collapsed in the Soviet Union and Eastern Europe. In China, Communists introduced limited free-market measures. New economic realities emerged, as people depended more than ever on goods, services, and ideas from other countries.

In studying this era, you should focus on the following questions:

✦ What were the causes and consequences of the Cold War?
✦ What problems do developing nations continue to face?
✦ What factors led to the collapse of Communism?
✦ What challenges does the world face in the post-Cold War era?

THE COLD WAR, 1945-1989

THE COLD WAR IN EUROPE

The **Cold War** was "cold" only in the sense that the two **superpowers**, both armed with nuclear weapons and missiles, never confronted one another in actual warfare.

THE ROOTS OF THE COLD WAR

The roots of the Cold War lay in two competing ideological systems: the United States

and other Western nations wanted to spread democracy and capitalism, while Soviet leaders promoted Communism. After World War II, the Soviet army continued to occupy Eastern Europe. Western leaders hoped that the nations of Eastern Europe would become free-market democracies, but Stalin turned them into Communist **satellites** (*puppet states*) so that the Soviet Union could never again be invaded from the West. By 1946, an **"Iron Curtain"** divided Europe: trade and communication between Eastern and Western Europe had been cut off.

GROWING AMERICAN INVOLVEMENT

With its strong economy and atomic bombs, America was the only country powerful enough to resist the Soviet Union. In 1947, Communist rebels threatened to take over Greece and Turkey. President Truman announced the **Truman Doctrine**, a plan which gave aid to Greece and Turkey to prevent takeovers. The U.S. then announced the **Marshall Plan**, in which America would give Western European nations billions of dollars to rebuild their war-torn economies so they could resist Communism. In 1948, the Soviets retaliated by closing all road and rail links leading to Berlin, in the Soviet-occupied part of Germany. The Western allies began a massive airlift to feed West Berliners, and the Soviets eventually backed down. In 1949, West Germany was formed out of the Western occupation zones. The U.S. and several European countries also formed **NATO** to protect Western Europe from Communist aggression. The Soviet Union responded by forming the **Warsaw Pact** with its Eastern European satellites in 1955.

THE COLD WAR REACHES ASIA

Just when the Western allies had stopped the spread of Communism in Europe through their "**containment**" policy, it appeared in Asia. In 1949, **Mao Zedong** and his Communist followers drove the government of **Chiang Kai-shek** out of China onto the island of Taiwan. Mao set up a dictatorship in which the Communist Party controlled every aspect of life, drastically changing traditional Chinese ways. Businessmen and wealthy peasants were killed, and farmlands were collectivized into large communes. Mao made himself into a god-like figure, similar to the emperors of ancient China.

Painting of Mao and his army on the "Long March" to victory in China

THE COLD WAR: 1950s - 1970s

In 1949, the Soviets tested their first atomic bomb. Soon each superpower developed hydrogen bombs and installed them on long-range missiles. However, American and Soviet leaders realized that the immensely destructive power of these weapons made them very dangerous to use. The superpowers had to find ways to compete other than by engaging in a nuclear war. They soon became involved in a number of lesser conflicts, sometimes leading to warfare on a limited scale.

THE KOREAN WAR, 1950-1953

In 1950, Communist North Korea invaded South Korea. The United States and other U.N. member countries intervened and drove the Communist North Koreans back to North Korea. In 1953 a compromise ended the war, leaving North and South Korea divided much as they had been before.

COMMUNISM IN CHINA

In China, Mao Zedong introduced the **Great Leap Forward,** a five-year plan meant to increase China's productivity and industrial power. China's Great Leap failed because of poor planning. By 1962, Mao had become concerned about the loss of enthusiasm for Communism among the common people. Mao announced a **Cultural Revolution.** He invited students to gather in Beijing and become **Red Guards.** The Red Guards traveled throughout China attacking writers, scientists, and professionals for abandoning Communist ideals. The Cultural Revolution took millions of lives and destroyed many historic monuments. China became so disrupted that Mao had to call out the army to control the Red Guards. In 1969, he sent them home, ending the Cultural Revolution.

THE SOVIET UNION AND EASTERN EUROPE

After Stalin died in 1953, Eastern Europeans began to demonstrate against Communist rule. When Hungarian leaders threatened to leave the Warsaw Pact in 1956, Soviet troops were sent into Hungary. Popular demonstrations were brutally repressed. In East Germany, large numbers of people were escaping to the West through Berlin. In 1961, Soviet leader **Nikita Khrushchev** sealed off the border between East and West Germany and ordered a wall built between East and West Berlin. For the next 28 years, the **Berlin Wall** served as a grim symbol of the Cold War.

COMMUNISM IN LATIN AMERICA: THE CUBAN REVOLUTION

In 1959, **Fidel Castro** seized power in Cuba. He nationalized businesses and executed opponents, transforming Cuba into a Communist state. Castro next threatened to export Communism to other Latin America nations. In 1961, Cuban exiles, armed and trained in America, unsuccessfully invaded Cuba at the **Bay of Pigs**. In 1962, American leaders discovered that Cuba was secretly building bases to install Soviet missiles with nuclear warheads. After President Kennedy ordered a naval blockade of Cuba and threatened an invasion, Khrush-

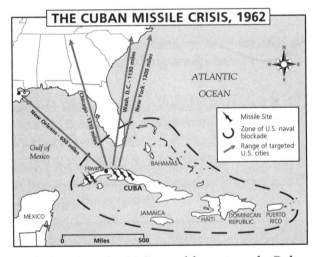

chev agreed to withdraw the missiles for a pledge that the U.S. would not invade Cuba.

THE WAR IN VIETNAM

When the French withdrew from Indochina in 1954, Vietnam was divided. **Ho Chi Minh** founded a Communist state in North Vietnam, while South Vietnam established ties to the West. Communists known as the **Vietcong** began a guerrilla war in South Vietnam, with North Vietnamese support. The U.S. entered the conflict to resist Communism. Although the U.S. used bombing and advanced technology, and sent in half a million soldiers, it could not defeat the North Vietnamese. In 1973, U.S. troops withdrew under the **Paris Peace Accords**. By 1975, South Vietnam fell to North Vietnam.

PROBLEMS OF THE DEVELOPING WORLD

While the superpowers were engaged in their deadly game of global rivalry, the nations of Africa, the Middle East, South Asia, and Latin America, known as the **Third World**, struggled with age-old problems of political instability and economic development.

AFRICA

Most newly independent African nations lacked democratic traditions. Many of their leaders assumed dictatorial powers in "one-party" states. A majority of Africans remained poor and lacked formal education. Africans struggled with problems of tribal conflict and political instability. The need for rapid economic development was the most pressing problem facing new African states. Standards of living in Africa were among the lowest in the world. One thing that united new African nations was their hostility to South Africa, which remained under the control of a white minority. In 1948, white South Africans began a policy of **apartheid** *(separating racial groups)*. Black South Africans resisted apartheid by both non-violent and violent means. In the 1970s, many countries cut their economic ties with South Africa in an attempt to force social change.

THE MIDDLE EAST

Zionism was a movement calling for Jews around the world to emigrate to Palestine, their ancient homeland. After the Holocaust, increasing numbers of Jews wanted to emigrate to Palestine. In 1948 the British left Palestine, which had been occupied by both Jews and Arabs for generations, and handed the problem to the United Nations. The U.N. voted to create the country of **Israel** as a Jewish homeland. The emergence of Israel as a Jewish state became a key political issue in the Middle East. Arab nations refused to recognize the new state. They attacked Israel, but were defeated. As a result of the war, many Palestinian Arabs fled from Israel and became refugees living in neighboring Arab lands. Wars erupted again in 1956, 1967, and 1973, with Israel the victor each time. In the 1967 war, Israel seized the Gaza Strip and Sinai Peninsula from Egypt, the West Bank from Jordan, and the Golan Heights from Syria.

THE CAMP DAVID ACCORDS

In 1978, Egyptian President **Anwar el-Sadat** and Israel's Prime Minister **Menachim Begin** met at Camp David with U.S. President Carter. They agreed that Israel would return lands taken from Egypt in exchange for peace between the two countries, ending thirty years of official hostility. Other Arab countries denounced the agreement.

ISRAEL AND THE PALESTINIANS

In 1964, Palestinian Arabs had formed the **Palestinian Liberation Organization**. The P.L.O. refused to recognize Israel and vowed to win back their homeland. In the 1960s and 1970s, the P.L.O. used terrorism as a political weapon. P.L.O. leaders felt they had no other way to oppose Israel. In 1987, young Palestinians who had grown up under Israeli occupation began a series of violent demonstrations, known as the **Intifada**. Israel used harsh measures to stop the protests, but with little success.

OPEC AND THE LEAP IN OIL PRICES

In the early 1970s, oil-producing countries formed **OPEC**. During the 1973 war with Israel, Arab OPEC members refused to sell oil to countries friendly to Israel, setting off a tremendous rise in oil prices. They kept prices high after the war. As a result, the West and non-oil-producing developing nations suffered high inflation and unemployment.

THE IRANIAN REVOLUTION AND ISLAMIC FUNDAMENTALISM

Shah Pahlavi, Iran's ruler in the post-war years, adopted Western culture and technology. In 1979, the Shah was overthrown by **Islamic Fundamentalists**. Reacting against Western culture and values, Islamic Fundamentalists believe in returning to the basic values of Islam. **Ayatollah Khomeini**, Iran's new ruler, established a constitution based on the Qu'ran. Women were required to return to traditional dress. Khomeini sponsored acts of terrorism, including the seizure of American hostages in Tehran.

SOUTH ASIA

After independence, South Asia faced problems typical of developing areas.

INDIA

In the 1960s and 1970s, the government improved food production by applying modern science to develop better seeds, fertilizers, and farming techniques, in the "**Green Revolution**." Increases in population often used up the gains in food production and industrial productivity. In an attempt to reduce high population growth, the government provided benefits to families limiting themselves to two children; however, despite this and other programs, India's population is still increasing at an alarming rate today. A steady stream of people flowing into India's cities has benefited industry but also created overcrowding and slums. Indian cultural differences have added to existing social problems. The government has attempted to prohibit discrimination against "Untouchables" and lower castes, but has only been partially successful.

BANGLADESH

When the Muslim state of Pakistan was formed in 1947, it consisted of two halves separated by nearly a thousand miles. In 1971, East Pakistan broke away from West Pakistan to become Bangladesh. Bangladesh suffers from periodic flooding and remains one of the world's poorest nations. Almost one-third of its children die before their fifth birthday. Most of its people cannot afford the most basic medical care.

LATIN AMERICA

Latin America faced a growing gulf between rich and poor, economic dependence on the West, and political instability. Military governments ruled many Latin American countries from the 1930s to the 1980s. These governments frequently violated people's basic human rights by imprisoning or executing suspected opponents without fair legal processes. The economic development of Latin America was hampered by a lack of capital for investment, an unskilled work force, and foreign competition. Many countries focused on producing single crops or minerals for export, like coffee or copper. Local elites invested their profits overseas instead of in their own countries. Population growth was so high that Latin America's population doubled every 25 years.

THE POST-COLD WAR PERIOD

In the Soviet Union, Eastern Europe and elsewhere, Communism came to an abrupt end at the close of the 1980s. The Berlin Wall came tumbling down, and new democracies emerged around the world. The post-Cold War period has proved to be a time of great optimism, even though new problems have appeared on the horizon.

THE COLLAPSE OF THE SOVIET UNION
AND THE LIBERATION OF EASTERN EUROPE

The most dramatic events of this era occurred in the Soviet Union. The sudden and unexpected collapse of Soviet Communism led directly to the end of the Cold War.

In 1985, **Mikhail Gorbachev** became leader of the Soviet Communist Party. Gorbachev wanted to preserve Communism, but sought to reform it. Gorbachev introduced **Glasnost** — greater "openness" — into Soviet society. Restrictions on speech and the press were lifted. Under **Perestroika** (*restructuring*), Gorbachev sought to introduce economic reforms by moving away from central planning and encouraging greater individual initiative in the Soviet economy. People were permitted to form small businesses, and factory managers were given greater control over production.

GORBACHEV'S PROBLEMS GROW

Gorbachev's policies failed to solve Soviet economic problems, and production continued to decline. His policies also unleashed forces of ethnic nationalism and social discontent. Non-Russian nationalities in the Soviet Union began demanding independence. The spirit of nationalism even spread to the Russian Republic itself. In 1991, **Boris Yeltsin** was elected President of the Russian Republic, and began to assert Russian authority over Gorbachev's Soviet government.

Boris Yeltsin

United Nations

THE BREAKUP OF THE SOVIET UNION (1991)

In August 1991, Communist hard-liners overthrew Gorbachev in a military **coup** *(sudden takeover of a government by force)*. Lacking popular support, however, the coup collapsed. Because many Communists had supported the coup, the Communist Party was discredited. In December 1991, Russia, Belarus, and Ukraine declared independence. These three states formed a new **Commonwealth of Independent States**. Other republics left the Soviet Union and joined the Commonwealth. The Soviet Union collapsed, and Gorbachev resigned at the end of 1991.

DISTRIBUTION OF FORMER SOVIET TERRITORIES

RUSSIAN REPUBLIC

76% of former Soviet land

24% of former Soviet land

ARMENIA
AZERBAIJAN
BELARUS
GEORGIA
ESTONIA
LATVIA
LITHUANIA
KAZAKHSTAN
KYRGYZSTAN
MOLDOVA
TURKMENISTAN
TAJIKISTAN
UKRAINE
UZBEKISTAN

RUSSIA SINCE 1991

Boris Yeltsin, President of the Russian Republic, quickly took drastic steps to reform its economy. He attempted to introduce the free market system by ending price controls on most goods and privatizing many state-owned industries. By 1993, the Russian Parliament, with many former Communists, feared Yeltsin was introducing changes too fast. Using military force, Yeltsin disbanded the Parliament when it tried to remove him from office; Yeltsin's supporters then won the next election. Yeltsin resigned in 1999, naming **Vladimir Putin** as his successor.

EASTERN EUROPE AND THE REUNIFICATION OF GERMANY

Even before the collapse of the Soviet Union, Gorbachev had allowed important changes to take place in Eastern Europe. These changes led to a lifting of the "Iron Curtain" between Western and Eastern Europe. The Berlin Wall, which had separated East and West Berlin since 1961, was knocked down in 1989. Throughout most of Eastern Europe, free elections brought non-Communist governments to power. One key event of the post-war period was the reunification of Germany. West Germany's leader, **Helmut Kohl**, negotiated the reunification which took effect at the end of 1990. After a half a century of division, Germany once again became a unified nation.

CHINA'S ECONOMIC REFORM

While Eastern Europe and the former Soviet Union struggled with political and economic change, China gradually introduced a free-market economy, without abandoning the Communist Party's monopoly of political power. In 1976, **Deng Xiaoping** became China's leader. His main goal was to modernize China by reforming its economy. Individuals were allowed to own small businesses. The private sector became responsible for a large portion of China's industrial output. China began producing more consumer goods, such as radios and television sets. New laws encouraged foreign investment, which brought capital and high-technology to special enterprise zones in China.

TIANANMEN SQUARE AND THE LIMITS OF REFORM

Although Chinese leaders encouraged economic reform, they retained the Communist political dictatorship. In 1989, university students demonstrated in **Tiananmen Square** in Beijing for greater freedom and democracy. When the students refused to disperse, tanks were brought in and fired on the demonstrators, killing hundreds. Others were later executed. In response, Western leaders reduced trade with China for a brief time. Since then, China has emerged as one of the world's fastest-growing economies. Deng Xiaoping died in 1997. His successor, **Jiang Zemin**, has generally followed his policies.

Tiananmen Square student demonstrators are paraded in a truck before being executed.

THE RESOLUTION OF OLD DISPUTES

The end of the Cold War placed new pressures on some of the world's problem areas.

ISRAEL AND THE MIDDLE EAST

At the **Middle East Peace Conference** in 1991, Israel's Prime Minister **Yitzhak Rabin** entered into negotiations with P.L.O. leader **Yassir Arafat**. In 1993, they reached an agreement in the **Oslo Accords**. Israel would give Palestinians self-government in the Gaza Strip and on the West Bank; in exchange, the P.L.O. would end its opposition to Israel's existence. In 1995, however, Rabin was assassinated by a Jewish opponent of the agreement. A **Palestinian Authority** was created, but subsquent terrorist acts and Israeli retaliation have stalled progress and greatly escalated tensions.

SOUTH AFRICA AND THE END OF APARTHEID

Responding to international pressures, white South Africans elected **F.W. De Klerk** as president. He ended apartheid and released **Nelson Mandela** and other political prisoners. He then negotiated with Mandela and other black leaders for a peaceful transition to a democratic government. In 1994, South Africa held its first multi-racial election. Nelson Mandela was elected as South Africa's first black president.

IRELAND'S RELIGIOUS CONFLICT

In 1922, Ireland became independent, but the Protestant majority in Northern Ireland chose to remain part of Great Britain. Many Catholics objected to the division of Ireland. Some formed the **Irish Republican Army (I.R.A.)**. In 1969, fighting erupted in Northern Ireland between the I.R.A. and the Northern Protestants. When the British sent in troops, open warfare was replaced by terrorism. In 1993, the British negotiated a cease-fire. In 1999 the Good Friday Agreement, a framework for solving Irish problems, was concluded, and the peace process has been moving slowly forward.

THE EMERGENCE OF NEW PROBLEMS

Today's new problems are fueled by ancient hatreds and conflicting economic interests.

FIGHTING IN YUGOSLAVIA

The liberation of Eastern Europe brought a revival of old ethnic rivalries in Yugoslavia. Croatia and Slovenia declared independence. Serb-dominated Yugoslavia responded by attacking Croatia. Fighting then erupted in Bosnia between Muslims and Serbs. Serb Yugoslavia intervened on behalf of the Bosnian Serbs. Some Bosnian Serbs began murdering Muslim civilians in what was called **"ethnic cleansing."**

After several years of civil war, the U.S. and other NATO countries finally stopped the fighting and imposed an uneasy truce. Bosnia was divided into two republics: Muslim and Serb. NATO subsequently bombed Yugoslavia when Serb troops attacked Albanian Muslims in the province of **Kosovo,** forcing Serb troops to retreat.

GENOCIDE IN AFRICA

Ethnic tensions erupted in **Rwanda** and **Burundi**. In 1994, the Hutu majority in Rwanda began to massacre the Tutsi minority. As many as half a million people, mostly Tutsi, were slain. Fighting even spread to nearby Congo and Uganda. In **Somalia**, on the northeastern "Horn" of Africa, a famine in 1990 was made worse by fighting among warlords, which kept people from receiving international aid. In 1992, the United States sent troops to Somalia to restore order and to protect food supplies. U.S. forces later withdrew when they could not stop the fighting among warlords.

IRAQ AND THE SECURITY OF THE PERSIAN GULF

Iraq occupies the lands of ancient Mesopotamia, where civilization first began. In 1979, **Saddam Hussein** seized power and imposed a brutal dictatorship on the people of Iraq. In 1980 he attacked Iran, leading to a bloody eight-year war.

In 1990, Hussein invaded neighboring Kuwait. Fearing an invasion of Saudi Arabia, the United States and other nations sent troops to expel the Iraqis from Kuwait. In the **Gulf War** that followed, Iraqi forces were quickly destroyed. Allied leaders nevertheless allowed Hussein to remain in power in Iraq. Soon after, Hussein's army attacked the Kurdish minority in northern Iraq.

Hussein failed to honor his agreement to permit United Nations inspectors to monitor Iraq to ensure that he was not stockpiling nuclear, biological or chemical weapons. After the terrorist attack on the United States on **September 11, 2001,** American and other world leaders insisted that Iraq show it was not hiding weapons of mass destruction (**WMD**). Some members of the U.N. Security Council urged delay, but the U.S., Britain and other allies invaded Iraq in March 2003. Saddam Hussein's government quickly collapsed. Following the liberation of Iraq from Hussein's rule, allied forces have faced rising violence and many other difficulties in trying to introduce democracy to Iraq.

AFGHANISTAN, THE TALIBAN AND AL QAEDA

Located in a mountainous region in the heart of Central Asia, Afghanistan achieved independence in the 1700s. In 1978, local Communists, with Soviet support, seized power. The countryside rebelled, and local guerrilla fighters with U.S. and other foreign support, overthrew Afghanistan's Communist government. Civil war among Afghanistan's various ethnic and religious groups followed.

The **Taliban,** a group of radical Muslim Fundamentalists, gradually gained control of the country. The Taliban imposed strict religious laws. Women were forbidden to appear in public without their bodies and faces being totally covered. They could not go to school or work. Men were not allowed to trim their beards. "Religious police" roamed the streets, beating those who disobeyed. The Taliban also allowed the Islamic terrorist group **al Qaeda,** led by Osama bin Laden, to operate training camps in Afghanistan. On September 11, 2001, al Qaeda terrorists hijacked U.S. jetliners and crashed them into the Pentagon and the World Trade Center. President Bush responded by declaring a **War on Terrorism.** When the Taliban refused to turn over bin Laden, the U.S. and its allies invaded Afghanistan. They overthrew the regime, and helped the Afghans form a democratic government.

THE NEW ECONOMIC REALITIES

With the end of the Cold War, most nations focused their energies on economic growth, the production of consumer goods, and the development of new technologies.

JAPAN'S ECONOMIC RECOVERY

At the end of World War II, Japan's industries and cities were in shambles. Yet by the 1970s, Japan was again a leading economic power. Athough it lacks natural resources, Japan profited from global interdependence by exporting huge amounts of high-tech goods. In the 1990s, however, Japan's economy experienced a slowdown.

ASIA'S NEW ECONOMIC GIANT: CHINA

Since opening its economy to foreign investment and technology, China has undergone an economic revolution. It obtained sovereignty over Hong Kong in 1997. After China joined the **World Trade Organization,** many restrictions on its exports were lifted. Its educated, low-wage workers have been a key factor in China's emergence as the world's fastest-growing economy.

FROM COMMON MARKET TO EUROPEAN UNION

In 1957, Germany and France formed the **Common Market,** the purpose of which was to eliminate tariffs among its members. In 1973, many other European nations joined. This created a huge free-trade zone in which goods, money, and people move freely. In 1991, the Common Market became the **European Union** (E.U.). In 1999, most E.U. nations agreed to a common currency called the "Euro." In May 2004, eight Eastern European countries joined the European Union.

SUMMARIZING YOUR UNDERSTANDING

OVERARCHING THEME

Events in one area of the world often affect developments in other parts of the world.

MAJOR IDEAS

BELIEF SYSTEMS
- The Cold War was a struggle between two competing belief systems.

ECONOMIC SYSTEMS
- The capitalist West was able to outperform the Communist bloc in the production of goods and services.
- Countries in Africa, Asia, and Latin America continue to struggle with problems of economic development.

POLITICAL SYSTEMS
- The failure of Communism has led to emerging democracies in some areas.

SCIENCE AND TECHNOLOGY
- Transportation and communication advances have created a "global village."

INTERDEPENDENCE
- Countries now depend upon one another for essential goods and services.

DIVERSITY
- Ethnic rivalries have proved more difficult to resolve than other problems.

IMPORTANT TERMS, CONCEPTS, AND PEOPLE

- ✦ Cold War
- ✦ Iron Curtain
- ✦ Truman Doctrine
- ✦ Marshall Plan
- ✦ NATO
- ✦ Korean War
- ✦ Great Leap Forward
- ✦ Cultural Revolution
- ✦ Mao Zedong

- ✦ Bay of Pigs Invasion
- ✦ Fidel Castro
- ✦ Ho Chi Minh
- ✦ Apartheid
- ✦ Camp David Accords
- ✦ P.L.O.
- ✦ OPEC
- ✦ Iranian Revolution
- ✦ Islamic Fundamentalism

- ✦ Green Revolution
- ✦ Glasnost and Perestroika
- ✦ Mikhail Gorbachev
- ✦ Tiananmen Square
- ✦ Irish Republican Army
- ✦ Nelson Mandela
- ✦ Persian Gulf War
- ✦ Saddam Hussein
- ✦ European Union (E.U.)

TESTING YOUR UNDERSTANDING

1   One similarity between imperial China and China under Communist rule is that both
    of them stressed
    1 state-supported religion   3 loyalty to leaders
    2 the importance of women in society   4 limited population growth

2   Mao's Great Leap Forward in China and Stalin's Five-Year Plans in the Soviet Union
    were similar in that they both attempted to increase their nation's
    1 private capital investment   3 religious tolerance
    2 individual ownership of land   4 industrial production

3   Which statement would be most consistent with the views of Fidel Castro in the 1960s?
    1 The spread of Communism is the greatest danger facing Latin America.
    2 A strong U.S. military presence is key to the defense of Latin America.
    3 Latin American progress can only be achieved through Communism.
    4 The free market system will improve the economies of Latin America.

4   In Africa, South Asia, and Latin America, people moved from villages to urban areas
    1 to avoid the high cost of living in rural areas
    2 to escape the poor climates of rural areas
    3 to find new jobs and improved educational opportunities
    4 to live among people of different ethnic backgrounds

5   The Cultural Revolution in China was Mao Zedong's attempt to
    1 renew the ideas and enthusiasm of the Communist revolution
    2 increase the industrial output of China
    3 promote artistic exchanges with the United States
    4 encourage foreign investment in China

6   During the 1970s, the government of the Shah in Iran came under major criticism by
    local religious leaders because of the
    1 war with Iraq   3 non-Islamic influences on their culture
    2 lack of rights for women   4 Shah's return to traditional Islamic law

7   The policies of Glasnost and Perestroika were introduced to the Soviet Union by
    1 Ayatollah Khomeini   3 Joseph Stalin
    2 Mikhail Gorbachev   4 Boris Yeltsin

8 The end of the Cold War was best symbolized by the
 1 establishment of the Truman Doctrine and the Marshall Plan
 2 formation of NATO and the European Common Market
 3 withdrawal of U.N. forces from Somalia and Kuwait
 4 destruction of the Berlin Wall and the reunification of Germany

9 The genocide in Rwanda and the atrocities in Yugoslavia demonstrate the
 1 inability of a command economy to satisfy the needs of people
 2 fact that most conflicts are caused by economic interests
 3 isolation of these countries from international influences
 4 inability of some societies to resolve religious and ethnic differences

10 One similarity between the leadership of the Meiji Emperor of Japan, Peter the Great
 of Russia, and the Shah of Iran was that they all supported policies that
 1 increased the power of the nobles   3 prevented industrial expansion
 2 introduced new religious beliefs   4 westernized their nations

THEMATIC ESSAY QUESTION

Directions: Write a well-organized essay that includes an introduction, several paragraphs explaining your position, and a conclusion.

Theme: Justice and Human Rights

> Throughout human history, certain groups have faced
> injustice, discrimination and brutality from those in power.

Task:

Choose *two* groups from your study of global history and geography.

For *each* group:
- Show how that group faced injustice or brutality from those in power.
- Explain how that group or the world community dealt with the injustice.

You may use any example from your study of global history and geography. Some sugges-
tions you might wish to consider include: Protestants during the Counter Reformation,
Native Americans living under European rule, Indians under British rule, Jews in Nazi
Germany, and black Africans under white South African rule.

You are *not* limited to these suggestions.

CHAPTER 12

GLOBAL CONCERNS

Essay questions on the Global History Regents Examination may ask about world problems or trends. This chapter provides an overview of some of these.

PROBLEMS

The world is changing rapidly. These changes have made nations more **interdependent** than ever before, and have helped to "shrink" the world into a **global village**. As the world has grown "smaller," problems in one part of the world have a greater impact on other parts of the world. In studying current problems, consider steps being taken to solve them. Also consider alternative viewpoints for attempting to resolve these problems.

OVERPOPULATION

In 1798, **Thomas Malthus** wrote that growing populations would always outstrip food supplies, condemning humankind to a cycle of population growth and decline through starvation. Today there six billion people in the world, and that number almost doubles every sixty years. Such growth often exceeds many developing nations' abilities to provide enough housing, water, and food for their expanding populations.

Possible Solutions. Many developing nations have adopted programs to limit their growth rate. In the 1970s, for example, China instituted a "one-child policy" for most families.

INTERNATIONAL TERRORISM

Terrorism is used as a weapon to draw attention to a group's grievances and to frighten governments into making concessions. Many radical groups in the world use terrorism for political ends. Terrorism reached new levels of destruction when members of the al Qaeda network hijacked airplanes and crashed them into the World Trade Center and the Pentagon on September 11, 2001.

Possible Solutions. Government responses to terrorism include negotiation, force, and retaliation. In 2001, President George W. Bush declared a **"War on Terrorism."** The United States and its allies invaded Afghanistan and overthrew the Islamic Fundamentalist Taliban government after it refused to surrender al Qaeda terrorists.

HUNGER AND MALNUTRITION

In much of the world, hunger and malnutrition are common. In developing nations, millions of young children go to bed hungry every night. Each advance in producing more food seems to be met by a corresponding increase in population.

Possible Solutions. Technological advances continue to be made for growing more food. The **Green Revolution** led to new high-yield crops and better fertilizers. Controlling population growth and protecting resources are the keys to reducing hunger.

ENVIRONMENTAL POLLUTION

Population growth and industrialization often cause increased pollution. Pollution creates such problems as **acid rain,** which destroys forests. Air pollution also appears to be making the Earth warmer. This **global warming** may have harmful consequences such as causing the polar ice caps to melt, which would raise sea levels. Another threat is the thinning of the **ozone layer**, which protects the Earth from the sun's radiation. Nuclear weapons and power plants pose special dangers to our environment. Nuclear waste can contaminate an area for millions of years. In 1986 a meltdown at **Chernobyl**, a Soviet nuclear power plant, caused radiation sickness over a wide area.

Possible Solutions. There is an increasing global awareness of the need to protect the environment. In 1992, 178 nations met at Rio de Janeiro in an **Earth Summit** devoted to achieving industrial growth without increasing world environmental problems. Since much pollution is caused by burning fossil fuels, there are increasing efforts to use alternative energy sources such as solar and wind power.

DEFORESTATION

The rain forests of Latin America, Africa, and South and Southeast Asia provide much of the oxygen we need for breathing. Some countries have been cutting down parts of their rain forests. Loss of rain forests also poses a threat to many endangered species.

Deforestation in Brazil

Possible Solutions. An international campaign is under way to save the world's rain forests. Measures include educating farmers about soil erosion, replanting trees, and restricting cattle grazing.

THE NORTH / SOUTH DICHOTOMY

About 3/4ths of the world's people live in **developing nations**. The gap between rich and poor nations keeps widening, and is sometimes referred to as the "North/South Dichotomy" *(division)*. The rich industrialized nations are called the "North" because most are in the Northern Hemisphere; the developing nations are called the "South."

Possible Solutions. Developing nations have tried a variety of strategies to promote economic development, including government control. Recently, developing nations have encouraged foreign investment and adopted free-market economies. International organizations like the **World Bank** help by providing loans and economic aid.

THE STATUS OF WOMEN

Traditionally, many societies barred women from holding property or participating in government. With the Industrial Revolution, more women entered the work force. After World War I, women in industrialized countries won the right to vote and other rights. Nevertheless, women still suffer inferior status in many parts of the world. In parts of Africa and Asia, they are subject to mutilation of their bodies when they reach adolescence. In some Islamic countries, women must wear veils, refrain from public appearances, and cannot drive cars. Even in Western countries, women are under-represented in politics and business, and on average earn less than men.

Possible Solutions. More women than ever before are attending colleges and entering professions such as medicine and law. International organizations attempt to prevent the worst abuses of women in the developing world — female mutilation, or the murder of infant girls where boys are preferred.

GLOBAL MIGRATION

After World War II large numbers of foreign workers entered Western Europe, where they filled low-paying jobs. Turks and Italians migrated to Germany, North Africans to France, and Pakistanis to Great Britain. Many of these "guest workers" were Muslims and were not accepted by Europeans as equals. Latin Americans and Asians have similarly migrated to the United States. In times of high unemployment, these workers are often resented and attacked by local groups.

Possible Solutions. In industrialized countries, many concerned citizens have condemned acts of violence against immigrants and reaffirmed the principles of equal rights for all. These countries have also taken steps to limit the number of refugees and other immigrants to a manageable level.

TRENDS

A **trend** is a pattern of change. Several patterns of change point the way to our future as a global community.

URBANIZATION AND MODERNIZATION

Urbanization means the movement of people into cities. Poverty in the Third World has driven millions of people to move to cities in search of jobs and education. Rising populations in cities require more food, heat, water, electricity, schools, and medical services than cities can provide. Rural newcomers also face **modernization** — the

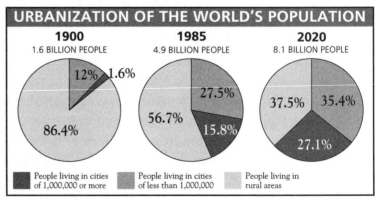

shedding of traditional beliefs in favor of modern ideas. Often cities are centers of modernization, creating social and psychological conflicts. Citizens in developing countries struggle to combine their traditional beliefs and values with modern ideas.

Third World governments are improving conditions in the countryside to slow the tide of migration, while providing more services, housing, and education in the cities. Population control can also help prevent further urban congestion.

SCIENTIFIC AND TECHNOLOGICAL CHANGE

We live in a time of constant scientific and technological change, which often creates social problems and cultural conflicts. We must make these new technologies serve genuine human needs, and provide people with support in adjusting to rapid change.

✦ **The Computer Revolution**. Today, computers that can perform millions of calculations in a few seconds are small enough to hold on one's lap. Some people have had problems adjusting to the computer revolution. Others fear that information stored in computers might lead to invasions of personal privacy.

✦ **Automation**. Computer-controlled robots work in factories that once needed skilled workers. This change provides cheaper products, but also reduces factory jobs. Some economists believe new jobs are created just as quickly as the old ones are eliminated, but in many fields workers find it hard to adjust.

✦ **Medical Advances**. Vaccines and antibiotics have wiped out many diseases. Major medical advances seem to occur almost on a daily basis. But medical costs are rising at an alarming rate. Many societies cannot afford modern health care.

✦ **Transportation**. Cars allow people to reach places in a short time that once took days to reach. However, the vast increase in the use of cars has caused smog, pollution, and clogged highways in cities throughout the world.

✦ **Communications**. Instant global communications among peoples has turned our world into a "global village." The Internet, a global network allowing computer users to exchange information quickly and cheaply, is increasing the information explosion still further. People are better informed today, but find it difficult to cope with ever-increasing amounts of information.

✦ **Space Exploration**. In 1957, the Soviets launched a satellite, Sputnik I, starting the "space race" between the Soviet Union and the U.S. The first men landed on the moon in 1969. Space exploration carries great national prestige, military advantages, and increased communication capabilities, but costs a vast amount of money.

TESTING YOUR UNDERSTANDING

1 The global problems of uneven economic development, environmental pollution, and hunger reflect the need for
   1 a return to policies of economic mercantilism
   2 increased military spending
   3 a reduction in the foreign aid provided by industrialized nations
   4 increased international cooperation

2 A valid statement about technology in the 20th century is that it has
   1 eliminated famine and disease throughout the world
   2 delayed economic progress in developing countries
   3 reduced the destructiveness of war
   4 accelerated the pace of cultural diffusion

3 Technological changes in developing countries have most often resulted in
   1 migrations from urban to rural areas   3 a weakening of traditional values
   2 fewer educational opportunities   4 a decreased use of natural resources

4 A study of the accident at the Chernobyl nuclear power plant in Ukraine and the severe air pollution in Mexico City would lead to the conclusion that
   1 technology can cause problems throughout the world
   2 international trade is more profitable than domestic commerce
   3 modern science cannot solve most political problems
   4 agricultural progress has caused major world environmental problems

5 Acid rain damage, contamination from nuclear accidents, and deterioration of the Earth's ozone layer indicate a need for
   1 the elimination of fossil fuels
   2 international cooperation and communication
   3 high tariffs and a favorable balance of trade
   4 nationalization of major industries

6 A major cause of the high birth rates in many developing nations has been
   1 the need for a large urban workforce
   2 a desire to counteract an increasing death rate
   3 a need to replace people killed during civil wars
   4 traditional beliefs and the economic need to have large families

7 One main concern regarding the destruction of rain forests in Latin America, Southeast Asia and sub-Saharan Africa is that
   1 cities will become seriously overcrowded
   2 it will lead to a decrease in the amount of oxygen in the atmosphere
   3 the per capita income in economically developing nations may increase
   4 water supplies in these areas will increase

8 The results of the destruction of rain forests in Brazil and the effects of acid rain on the forests of North America and Europe demonstrate that
   1 the nations of the world have been successful in protecting the environment
   2 activities in one region can adversely affect another region's environment
   3 each nation must act alone to solve its environmental problems
   4 natural resources are scarce throughout the world

9 Many scientists believe that global warming is the result of
   1 overgrazing on land in developing nations
   2 burning large amounts of gasoline, oil, and coal in developed nations
   3 testing nuclear weapons in violation of the Nuclear Test Ban Treaty
   4 using new fertilizers to increase crop production

THEMATIC ESSAY QUESTION

Directions: Write a well-organized essay that includes an introduction, several paragraphs explaining your position, and a conclusion.

Theme: Interdependence

> Global concerns pose challenges for both national and international efforts.

Task:

Choose **two** global concerns from your study of global history and geography.

> For *each* global concern:
> • Describe why it is considered to be a problem.
> • Show how the problem might be resolved.

You may use any example from your study of global history and geography. Some suggestions you may wish to consider include: pollution, terrorism, desertification, overpopulation, and hunger.

You are *not* limited to these suggestions.

A FINAL REVIEW

Congratulations — you have just reviewed more than 3,000 years of global history! At this point you may be wondering how you will remember all of the events, people, and dates you just read about. This chapter contains five sections for a helpful final review:

❖ **Section 1: Major Concepts.** This section provides a glossary of the most important concepts in global history.

❖ **Section 2: Major Terms.** This section is a checklist of the major terms you need to know. Each entry lists the page number on which the term is first explained.

❖ **Section 3: Major People.** This section provides a checklist of the major people you should know about, and the page number on which the person is first identified.

❖ **Section 4: Study Organizers.** This section provides study organizers for you to complete that bring together what you have learned by *theme*, such as major historical turning points, important revolutions, and major religions.

❖ **Section 5: Area Study Guides.** This section presents a series of study guides organized chronologically by *region*. These guides help you trace developments in each part of the world, to review what you have learned from a different perspective.

SECTION 1: GLOSSARY OF MAJOR CONCEPTS

Absolutism: The complete control of a monarch over his subjects, closely associated with divine right. Louis XIV of France was an example of an absolute ruler.

Capitalism: An economic system characterized by the private ownership of property. Capital is invested in the hope of creating wealth for the entrepreneur — the individual who risks the money. Consumers choose to buy or not buy what is produced.

Communism: Communists believe eliminating private property ends class struggle and leads to an ideal society. In practice, Communism has been characterized by government control of all aspects of production and distribution.

Cultural Diffusion: The spread of ideas and products from one culture to another.

Decolonization. The process by which European colonies in Africa and Asia became independent states after World War II.

Democracy: A system in which citizens participate in government decisions either by voting directly on issues brought before them or by electing people to represent them. Democracy was first developed in Athens around the 5th century B.C.

Dictatorship: A system in which citizens have few rights and the government is controlled by an individual or small group. For example, Nazi Germany under Adolf Hitler and the Soviet Union under Joseph Stalin were dictatorships.

Fascism: European political movement that emerged in 1919-1939. Fascists believed that the state is supreme, that an absolute leader best expresses the state's needs, and citizens must sacrifice for the state. Nazi Germany and Fascist Italy were Fascist states.

Global Interdependence: In an interdependent world, each nation depends on selling and buying goods and services from other nations.

Imperialism (colonialism): The control of one area or country by another. In the late 1800s, European imperialism led to European control of much of Africa and Asia.

Mercantilism: An economic theory that a nation's wealth could be measured by the amount of its gold and silver. In the 1600s and 1700s, mercantilists urged European rulers to acquire colonies and export manufactured goods.

Nationalism: The belief that each ethnic group or "nationality" is entitled to its own government and national homeland.

Totalitarianism: A system in which a dictatorial government controls all aspects of life: education, ideas, the economy, music, and art. Citizens lack individual rights.

Urbanization : People moving from rural areas to cities for jobs and new opportunities.

Westernization: Non-Western countries imitating Western European customs and technology. Peter the Great "Westernized" Russia in the 1700s and Japan adopted similar "Westernizing" policies in the late 1800s.

SECTION 2: CHECKLIST OF MAJOR TERMS

❐ Apartheid (96)
❐ Appeasement (85)
❐ Aztecs (56)
❐ Balance of Power (68)
❐ Black Death (50)
❐ Bolsheviks (82)
❐ Boxer Rebellion (72)
❐ Buddhism (29)
❐ Bushido (50)
❐ Byzantine Empire (40)
❐ Camp David Accords (96)
❐ Caste System (29)
❐ Chernobyl (108)
❐ Code of Hammurabi (20)
❐ Cold War (93)
❐ Collective farms (83)
❐ Commercial Revol. (59)
❐ Communism (69)
❐ Confucianism (30)
❐ Congress of Vienna (68)
❐ Council of Trent (51)
❐ Crusades (42)
❐ Cuban Missile Crisis (95)
❐ Cuban Revolution (95)
❐ Cultural Revolution (92)
❐ Deforestation (109)
❐ Developing Nations (109)
❐ Divine Right Theory (59)
❐ Enlightenment (61)
❐ Ethnic cleansing (101)
❐ European Union (102)
❐ Feudalism (42)
❐ Five Year Plans (83)
❐ Fourteen Points (81)
❐ French Revolution (67)
❐ Genocide (86)
❐ Glasnost (98)
❐ Global Warming (108)
❐ Great Leap Forward (94)

❐ Green Revolution (97)
❐ Gulf War (102)
❐ Gupta Empire (29)
❐ Hinduism (30)
❐ Hiroshima (86)
❐ Holocaust (86)
❐ Huang He (22)
❐ Inca Empire (56)
❐ Indus Riv. Valley Civ. (21)
❐ Industrial Revolution (69)
❐ Intifada (97)
❐ I.R.A. (101)
❐ Iranian Revolution (97)
❐ Islam (40)
❐ Islamic Fundamental. (97)
❐ Judaism (22)
❐ Kingdom of Ghana (48)
❐ Kingdom of Mali (48)
❐ Kingdom of Songhai (48)
❐ Kush (22)
❐ Laissez-faire (69)
❐ League of Nations (82)
❐ Mandate of Heaven (29)
❐ Marshall Plan (93)
❐ Maurya Empire (29)
❐ Maya (56)
❐ Meiji Restoration (72)
❐ Mesopotamia (20)
❐ Mexican Rev. of 1910 (80)
❐ Middle Ages (41)
❐ Ming Dynasty (62)
❐ Mongols (49)
❐ Monotheism (22)
❐ Mughals (62)
❐ NATO (93)
❐ Nazism (84)
❐ Neolithic Revolution (20)
❐ Ninety-Five Theses (51)
❐ Nuremberg Trials (86)

❐ OPEC (97)
❐ Open Door Policy (72)
❐ Ottoman Empire (61)
❐ P.L.O. (97)
❐ Perestroika (97)
❐ Qin Dynasty (29)
❐ Qing *(Manchu)* Dynasty (62)
❐ Qu'ran *(Koran)* (41)
❐ Reformation (51)
❐ Reign of Terror (67)
❐ Renaissance (51)
❐ Roman Empire (28)
❐ Russian Revolution (82)
❐ Russification (70)
❐ Salt March (87)
❐ Savanna (48)
❐ Scientific Revolution (60)
❐ Sepoy Mutiny (71)
❐ Shogun (50)
❐ Silk Road (28)
❐ Social Darwinism (71)
❐ Steppes (49)
❐ Sung Dynasty (43)
❐ Superpowers (93)
❐ T'ang Dynasty (43)
❐ Terrorism (108)
❐ Tiananmen Sq. Protest (100)
❐ Tokugawa Shogunate (72)
❐ Transatlantic slave trade (58)
❐ Treaty of Versailles (81)
❐ Truman Doctrine (93)
❐ United Nations (86)
❐ Urbanization (110)
❐ Vietnam War (95)
❐ Warsaw Pact (93)
❐ Weimar Republic (84)
❐ World War I (80)
❐ World War II (85)
❐ Young Turks (80)

SECTION 3: CHECKLIST OF MAJOR PEOPLE

ASIAN POLITICAL LEADERS
❑ Asoka the Great (273-238 B.C.) 29
❑ Kublai Khan (1215-1294) 49
❑ Akbar the Great (1542-1605) 62
❑ Sun Yat-sen (1866-1925) 80
❑ Ho Chi Minh (1890-1969) 95
❑ Mao Zedong (1893-1976) 94
❑ Mohandas Gandhi (1869-1948) 87
❑ Deng Xiaoping (1904-1996) 100

AFRICAN POLITICAL LEADERS
❑ Mansa Musa (1270-1332) 48
❑ Jomo Kenyatta (1894-1978) 87
❑ Kwame Nkrumah (1909-1972) 89
❑ Nelson Mandela (1918-present) 101

EUROPEAN POLITICAL LEADERS
❑ Alexander the Great (356-323 B.C.) 28
❑ Charlemagne (742-814) 42
❑ Peter the Great (1672-1725) 60
❑ Catherine the Great (1729-1796) 60
❑ Napoleon Bonaparte (1769-1821) 68
❑ Otto von Bismarck (1815-1898) 70
❑ Vladimir Lenin (1870-1924) 82
❑ Joseph Stalin (1879-1953) 83
❑ Adolf Hitler (1889-1945) 84
❑ Mikhail Gorbachev (1931-present) 98

MIDDLE EASTERN POLITICAL LEADERS
❑ Anwar el-Sadat (1918-1981) 96
❑ Shah Pahlavi (1919-1980) 97

LATIN AMERICAN POLITICAL LEADERS
❑ Simon Bolivar (1783-1830) 69
❑ Fidel Castro (1927-present) 95

RELIGIOUS LEADERS
❑ Siddartha Gautama (563 -483 B.C.) 30
❑ Confucius (551-479 B.C.) 30
❑ Jesus (1-30 A.D.) 30
❑ Mohammed (570-632) 40
❑ Martin Luther (1483-1546) 51
❑ Ayatollah Khomeini (1900-1996) 97

THINKERS, WRITERS, SCIENTISTS, AND INVENTORS
❑ Johann Gutenberg (1398-1468) 51
❑ Nicolaus Copernicus (1437-1543) 51
❑ Nicolo Machiavelli (1469-1527) 51
❑ John Locke (1632-1704) 60
❑ Isaac Newton (1642-1727) 60
❑ Charles Darwin (1809-1882) 71
❑ Karl Marx (1818-1883) 69
❑ Friedrich Engels (1820-1895) 69

SECTION 4: STUDY ORGANIZERS

IMPORTANT CIVILIZATIONS

The rise and fall of civilizations is a major theme of global history. Summarize your knowledge by completing this organizer. The first item has been done as a model.

Civilization	Location	Major Characteristics	Reasons For Its Rise or Fall
River Valley Civilizations	*Egypt, Mesopotamia, Indus River, Huang He*	*The first civilizations in which people lived in cities and developed writing systems.*	*Rivers deposited rich soils during annual floods, allowing farmers to grow surplus crops. This made possible the rise of civilizations.*
Roman Empire			
Dynastic China			
Byzantine Empire			
Arab Islamic Empire			
Meso-american Civilizations			
West African Kingdoms			

MAJOR BELIEF SYSTEMS

Belief systems have had a major impact on the lives of people as well as on global history. Summarize your knowledge of belief systems by completing the following study organizer:

Belief System	Where It Was Found	Major Beliefs or Practices
Judaism		
Confucianism		
Christianity		
Buddhism		
Hinduism		
Islam		
Islamic Fundamentalism		

TURNING POINTS IN HISTORY

A number of significant milestones have had a profound impact on global history. Summarize your knowledge of these by completing the following study organizer.

Turning Point	Describe It	Its Impact on the World
Golden Age of Greece (5th century B.C.)		
Fall of Rome (476 A.D.)		
Birth of Islam (622-632)		
Mongol Conquests (1200s)		
Fall of Constantinople (1453)		
European Encounter w/ the Americas (1492)		
Protestant Reformation (1517)		
Meiji Restoration (1868)		
Russian Revolution (1917)		
Atom Bomb Dropped on Japan (1945)		
Indian Independence (1947)		
Dissolution of the Soviet Union (1991)		

FORMS OF GOVERNMENT

Throughout history, people have lived under different systems of governments. Summarize your knowledge of governments by completing this study organizer.

Form of Government	Major Ideas or Features	Examples
Democracy		
Feudalism		
Absolutism		
Fascism		
Totalitarianism		

TYPES OF ECONOMIC SYSTEMS

Throughout history, people have organized their economies to meet their needs. Summarize your knowledge of economic systems by completing this study organizer.

Economic System	Major Features	Example
Traditional		
Mercantilist		
Capitalist		
Communist		

MAJOR REVOLUTIONS

Certain events in history have brought about great changes in government, ideas, or society with amazing speed. Summarize your knowledge of some of these major revolutions by completing the following study organizer.

Revolution	Where	When	Effects / Changes / Impacts
Neolithic Revolution			
Commercial Revolution			
Scientific Revolution			
French Revolution			
Industrial Revolution			
Russian Revolution			
Chinese Revolution			
Cuban Revolution			
Iranian Revolution			

SECTION 5: AREA STUDY GUIDES

The following five pages contain reviews of events, in chronological order, in six major areas of the world: the Middle East and North Africa, Asia, the Americas, Sub-Saharan Africa, Europe, and Russia and the former Soviet Union.

THE MIDDLE EAST AND NORTH AFRICA

EARLY CIVILIZATION 10,000 BC - 500 BC	A NEW CENTER OF CULTURE 330 - 1453	ISLAMIC EXPANSION 570 - 1770	OTTOMAN EMPIRE 1453 - 1918	MIDDLE EAST IN THE 20TH CENTURY 1900 - PRESENT

EARLY HUMAN SOCIETY
• Neolithic Revolution
 	
RIVER VALLEY CIVILIZATIONS
• Mesopotamia
  —Fertile Crescent
  —Tigris and Euphrates Rivers
  —Sumerians
  —Code of Hammurabi
• Ancient Egypt
  —Pyramids
  —Pharoahs
  —Hieroglyphics
• The Hebrews
  —Judaism
  —Monotheism
  —Ten Commandments
  —Exodus
• Phoenicians
  —First alphabet
 	
PERSIA (550–100 BC)
• large empire uniting many peoples
• Cyrus the Great
• Zoroastrianism
• attempted conquest of Greek city-states
	BYZANTINE EMPIRE
	• Continuation of east Roman Empire
	  —Emperor Constantine
	  —Constantinople
	• Legacy of Byzantium
	  —Code of Justinian
	  —Eastern Orthodox Christianity
	  —Hagia Sophia
		RISE OF ISLAM
		• Arose in Arabia
		• Mohammed
		  —Allah
		  —Qu'ran (Koran)
		  —Hegira and Jihad
		• Five Pillars of Faith
		  —Confession of Faith
		  —Pray 5 times a day
		  —Charity
		  —Fasting during Ramadan
		  —Pilgrimage to Mecca
		• Golden Age of Islamic Rule
		  —Abbasid Caliphate
		
		CRUSADES (1096)
		• Seljuk Turks
		• Attempt to regain Holy Land
		• Cultural diffusion
			OTTOMAN TURK EXPANSION
			• Took Constantinople
			• Suleiman the Magnificent
			• Toleration of Jews and Christians
			
			SAFAVID EMPIRE
			• Persia
			  —Ruled by Shahs
			  —Persian carpets
			
			DECLINE OF THE OTTOMAN EMPIRE
			• Disunity
			• Warfare with Persia, Austria, Russia
			• Failure to modernize
			• Loss of Territories (Balkans, Egypt)
			
			TRANSFORMATION INTO MODERN TURKEY
			• Young Turks (1908)
			• Ottoman empire sides with Germany in World War I
			• Creation of modern Turkey under Kemal Atatürk
				RISE OF NATIONALISM
				• British and French mandates
				• Independent states emerge
				• Pan Arab Movement
				
				ARAB-ISRAELI CONFLICT
				• Zionism
				• War of Independence (1948)
				• Further Wars, 1956/1967/ 1973
				• Continued Tensions
				  —Camp David Accords
				  —P.L.O./Intifada
				• Mideast Peace Conference
				  —Palestinian Authority
				
				OTHER HOT SPOTS
				• OPEC and Middle East Oil
				• Iranian Revolution
				  —Islamic Fundamentalism
				  —Ayatollah Khomeini
				• Iraq and Saddam Hussein
				  —Iran-Iraq War
				  —Kuwait invaded
				  —First Gulf War, 1990
				  —Second Gulf War, 2003
				• Sept. 11, 2001 terror attacks on U.S. by al Qaeda
				• U.S. overthrows Taliban in Afghanistan

☐ASIA

EARLY CIVILIZATAIONS 2500 BC - 500 AD	STABILITY AND CHANGE 500 - 1900	TWENTIETH CENTURY 1900 - PRESENT

EARLY CIVILIZATAIONS 2500 BC - 500 AD

CHINA
- Huang He Valley (2000—1027 BC)
- Shang Dynasty (1760—1027 BC)
- Zhou Dynasty (1027—221 BC)
  - —Mandate of Heaven
  - —Confucius
  - —Lao Tzu and Daoism
- Qin Dynasty (221 BC-206 BC)
  - —Shi-Huangdi was first emperor
  - —Great Wall of China built
- Han Dynasty (206 BC-220 AD)
  - —Silk Road
  - —Examinations for imperial service
- Period of Disunity
  - —Warfare among kingdoms for control of China
  - —Longest period of disunity in Chinese history

INDIA
- Indus River Valley (2500—1500 BC)
  - —Harappans
- Aryan Invasions
  - —Hinduism
  - —Caste system
  - —Buddhism
- Mauryan Empire (321 BC-232 AD)
  - —Asoka
- Gupta Empire (320-535)
  - —Golden Age of Hindu Culture
  - —Hun invasions

STABILITY AND CHANGE 500 - 1900

CHINA
- T'ang Dynasty (618—907)
  - —Golden Age: reunited China
  - —Expansion into Korea and Manchuria
- Sung Dynasty (960—1279)
  - —Golden Age: the compass, gunpowder
- Yuan Dynasty (1279—1368)
  - —Mongol conquest
  - —Kublai Khan
  - —Marco Polo visits
- Ming Dynasty (1368—1644)
  - —Middle Kingdom
- Qing (Manchu) Dynasty (1644—1912)
  - —Opium War
  - —Spheres of Influence
  - —Boxer Rebellion (1899)

JAPAN
- Chinese influence on Japan
  - —Writing, Confucianism, Buddhism
- Heian Period (794—1185)
  - —Golden Age: Tale of Genji
- Shogunates (1200—1550)
  - —Japanese feudalism
  - —Shoguns, Daimyos, Samurai
  - —Tokugawa Shogunate
- Meiji Restoration (1868—1912)
  - —Adoption of Western ways

INDIA
- Muslim Invasions
- Mughal Empire (1526—1837)
  - —Akbar the Great
  - —Shah Jahan, Taj Mahal
- British Rule (1800s—1947)
  - —British East India Company

TWENTIETH CENTURY 1900 - PRESENT

CHINA
- Republican Period (1912—1949)
  - —Sun Yat-Sen and Three Principles
  - —Chiang Kai-Shek and the Kuomintang
  - —Japanese invasion (1937—1945)
- Communist Period (1949—Present)
  - —Two Chinas: Mainland China and Taiwan
  - —Mao Zedong
  - —Red Guards and Cultural Revolution
  - —Deng Xiaoping
  - —Jiang Zemin

JAPAN
- Rise to Power (1900—1930s)
  - —Russo-Japanese War
  - —Sino-Japanese War
  - —World War I
- World War II (1935—1945)
  - —Pearl Harbor
  - —Hiroshima and Nagasaki
  - —U.S. Occupation of Japan
  - —Constitution of 1947
- Rise to Economic Power (1970—Present)
  - —Economic Superpower

INDIA/SOUTHEAST ASIA
- Independence Movements
  - —Mohandas Gandhi, India
  - —Ho Chi Minh, Vietnam
- Partition of India (1947)
  - —Pakistan & India
  - —Bangladesh Independence (1971)
- Cold War in Asia
  - —Korean War (1951—1952)
  - —Vietnam War (1965—1974)

THE AMERICAS

PRE-COLUMBIAN CIVILIZATIONS 30,000 BC - 1546 AD	EUROPEAN COLONIALISM 1500 - 1850	RECENT HISTORY 1800 - PRESENT
MIGRATIONS FROM ASIA (30,000 B.C—10,000 BC) • Settlers cross Bering Strait to the Americas **OLMECS** • One of first known Mexican civilizations **MAYA CIVILIZATION** (1500 BC—1546 AD) • In Guatemala; later Yucatan • Agricultural, grew corn • Perfected calendar • Human sacrifices **AZTEC EMPIRE** (1200—1521) • Controlled Central Mexico • Rigid social structure • Human sacrifices to Sun God **INCA EMPIRE** (1200—1535) • Along Andes Mountains • Rigid class structure • Grew potatoes, root crops • Built stone roads and stone buildings • Developed writing & number systems • Built large cities with pyramids, palaces —*Machu Picchu*	**EUROPEAN CONQUEST** (1492—1542) • Arrival of conquistadors • Cortés defeats Aztecs (1521) —*Montezuma* • Pizarro defeats Incas (1535) **EFFECTS OF CONQUEST** • New foods and products introduced to Europe • Diseases devastated native populations • Spread of Christianity • Spanish and Portuguese culture to Latin America **THE COLONIAL EXPERIENCE** • Rule of Spain and Portugal • Encomienda (hacienda) system • Colonial social classes —*Peninsulares* —*Creoles* —*Mestizos, mulattos* —*Natives and Africans* • Mercantilism	**INDEPENDENCE MOVEMENTS** • Causes —*Examples of French and American Revolutions* —*Weakening of Spain* • Independence leaders —*Haiti: Toussaint L'Ouverture* —*Venezuela, Colombia: Simón Bolívar* —*Mexico: Miguel Hidalgo* **19TH CENTURY** • Monroe Doctrine (1823) stopped new colonization • Rule of the Caudillos **20TH CENTURY** • Mexican Revolution of 1910 —*Díaz and Pancho Villa* —*Mexican Constitution* • Cuban Revolution (1959) —*Castro* —*Communism* —*Bay of Pigs Invasion* —*Cuban Missile Crisis* • Nicaraguan Revolution (1979) —*Sandinistas vs. Contras* • Military dictatorships • Debts to Western banks • Problems of economic development

SUB-SAHARAN AFRICA

EARLY HISTORY 750 BC - 1800 AD	RECENT HISTORY 1800 - PRESENT
KUSH (750 BC—350 A.D) • Important iron producer • Rich from ivory, ebony • Egyptian cultural influence • Developed its own writing **KINGDOM OF GHANA** (750-1200) • Rich from gold-salt trade • Captives used as slaves **KINGDOM OF MALI** (1240-1400) • Rich from gold-salt trade • Kings adopted Islam —*Mansa Musa* —*Timbuktu: center of learning* **KINGDOM OF SONGHAI** (1464-1600) • Founded by Sultan Sunni Ali • Islamic kingdom • Grew rich from trade **OTHER AFRICAN STATES** • Benin • Great Zimbabwe • Coastal cities of East Africa • Ethiopia **TRANSATLANTIC SLAVE TRADE** • Greatly expanded slave trade • About 15 million Africans enslaved in 300 years • Many died en route • Disrupted African development	**CAUSES OF NEW IMPERIALISM** • Expanded technology • Economic motives • National pride • Balance of power • Other motives —*Social Darwinism* **SCRAMBLE FOR AFRICA** • British take Egypt • Berlin Conference, 1884-85 • Boer War in South Africa **DECOLONIZATION** • Rise of nationalism • World War II weakened European control • Independence movements —*Kwame Nkrumah* —*Jomo Kenyatta* • Single-party states • Problems of economic development **MODERN-DAY AFRICA** • South Africa —*Apartheid* —*Nelson Mandela* —*F.W. DeKlerk* • Tribalism —*Rwanda and Burundi* • Hunger and famine —*Somalia* • Shift to democratic governments

EUROPE

CLASSICAL CIVILIZATIONS 1000 BC - 500 AD	MIDDLE AGES AND RENAISSANCE 500 - 1500	BIRTH OF THE MODERN WORLD 1500 - 1770	NEW CURRENTS 1770 - 1900	THE WORLD AT WAR 1900 - 1945	ATOMIC AGE 1945 - Present
GREEKS • City-States —Sparta —Athens • Persian War • Golden Age —Pericles —Parthenon —Democracy • Achievements —philosophy —sculpture —drama —history • Hellenistic Period —Alexander the Great **ROMANS** • Roman Republic —12 Tables of Roman Law —Julius Caesar • Roman Empire —Augustus —Pax Romana —Rise of Christianity • Decline —economic problems —division into East and West Rome —barbarian invasions	**BYZANTINE EMPIRE** • East Roman Empire • Constantinople • Eastern Orthodox Christianity • Preserved classical learning **CHAOS IN WEST** • Barbarian invasions • Rise of the Franks • Charlemagne • Viking Invasions **FEUDAL SOCIETY** • Lords/knights • Serfs/manors • Age of Faith —Catholic Church —Crusades **DECLINE OF FEUDALISM** • Black Death • Rise of towns • Use of money **RENAISSANCE** • Italian city-states • Humanists • Key people —Leonardo da Vinci —Michelangelo —Machiavelli —Gutenberg	**REFORMATION** • Corruption in Church • Martin Luther • Wars of religion • Catholic Counter Reformation —Jesuits —Council of Trent **AGE OF DISCOVERY** • Explorers • Conquest of Americas • New foods to Europe **EUROPE'S CONQUEST OF AMERICAS** • Cortés/Aztec Civiliz. • Pizarro/Inca Civiliz. **COMMERCIAL REVOLUTION** • Mercantilism • Capitalism **AGE OF KINGS** • Rise of royal power • Divine Right —Absolutism **LIMITED MONARCHY** • Magna Carta • Rise of Parliament —English Revolution —Bill of Rights (1689)	**SCIENTIFIC REVOLUTION** • Scientific Method —Galileo and Newton **ENLIGHTENMENT** • Belief in natural law —Locke and Voltaire —Rousseau **FRENCH REVOLUTION** • Causes • Highlights —Estates General —National Assembly • Reign of Terror • Rise of Napoleon • Congress of Vienna **INDUSTRIAL REVOLUTION** • Starts in Britain • Reform movements • Communism —Marx/Engels **NATIONALISM** • Revolutions of 1848 • Italy unified —Count Cavour • Germany unified —Otto von Bismarck **IMPERIALISM** • India, Africa, China, Indochina	**WORLD WAR I** • Causes —Nationalism —Alliance system —Militarism • Major Events —Trench warfare • Aftermath —Versailles Treaty —League of Nations **INTERWAR YEARS** • Prosperity • Depression • Rise of Fascism —Hitler/Nazis —Mussolini **WORLD WAR II** • Causes —Nazi aggression • Major Events —Blitzkrieg —Battle of Britain —Invasion of Russia —Holocaust —Atom bomb • Aftermath —Nuremberg Trials —U.N. created —Germany divided	**SUPERPOWER RIVALRY** • U.S. vs. Soviet Union • Cold War —Truman Doctrine —Marshall Plan —Berlin Wall • NATO vs. Warsaw Pact **END OF COLD WAR** • Policy of détente • Freedom for Eastern Europe —Lech Walesa —Solidarity • Reunification of Germany —Berlin Wall knocked down —Helmut Kohl • Dissolution of USSR **EUROPE TODAY** • Common Market to European Union • Ethnic and religious conflicts —Bosnia —Northern Ireland • Immigration policies • Pollution • Economic problems of Eastern Europe

RUSSIA AND THE FORMER SOVIET UNION

EARLY HISTORY 800 A.D. - 1917 A.D.	A COMMUNIST STATE 1917 - 1991	MOVE TO DEMOCRACY 1991 - PRESENT

STATE OF KIEV (800s–1240)
• Vikings organized the Slavs into a kingdom
• Byzantine influence
 	
MONGOL CONTROL (1240–1480)
 	
RISE OF MUSCOVY (1480–1598)
 	
ROMANOV RULE (1613–1917)
• Peter the Great (1682–1725)
  –Westernization
  –Expansion
• Catherine the Great (1762–1796)
  –Continued Westernization
  –Acquisition of Turkish and Polish lands
  –Serf conditions worsen
• Autocratic Russia
  –Absolute rulers
  –Defeat of Napoleon
  –Crimean War
  –Tsar Alexander II
  –Emancipation of the Serfs
  –Russification
  –Pogroms against Jews
 	
RUSSIAN REVOLUTION OF 1905
• Nicholas II grants limited reforms
	RUSSIAN REVOLUTION OF 1917
	• Russia unprepared for World War I
	• Overthrow of Tsar Nicholas II
	• Bolsheviks take power
	• Russia withdraws from World War I
	
	RULE BY LENIN (1917–1924)
	• Introduces Communism
	  –Civil War: Reds vs. Whites
	  –New Economic Plan (N.E.P.)
	
	RULE BY STALIN (1924–1953)
	• Totalitarianism: purges, gulags
	• Economic Changes
	  –Collectivization
	  –Five Year Plans: from agriculture to industry
	• World War II
	  –Non-aggression treaty with Germany
	  –Joins Allies against Germany
	
	COLD WAR (1945–1991)
	• Democracy vs. Communism
	• Occupation of Eastern Europe
	  –Soviet Satellites
	  –Iron Curtain
	• U.S. Response: Marshall Plan and Truman Doctrine
	• Division of Germany
	• NATO vs. Warsaw Pact
	• Khrushchev (1953–1965)
	  –Denounces Stalinism
	  –Cuban Missile Crisis
	• Brezhnev (1965–1982)
	  –Stagnation of Soviet economy
	  –Détente
		GORBACHEV (1985–1991)
		• Reform policies
		  –Glasnost (greater openness)
		  –Perestroika (restructuring)
		  –New foreign Policy
		• Gorbachev's reforms fail
		  –unfamiliar with free market system
		  –opposed by party bureaucrats
		  –political instability
		  –declining industrial production
		• Rising nationalism
		  –Baltic States
		  –Russia
		  –Treaty of Union
		• Coup of August 1991
		• Dissolution of the Soviet Union, December 1991
		
		COMMONWEALTH OF INDEPENDENT STATES (1991–Present)
		• Association of independent states
		• Importance of the Russian Republic
		• Yeltsin introduces changes
		  –Democracy
		  –Free Market System

A FINAL TEST

Now that you have reviewed test-taking strategies and the global history content areas, you should measure your progress by taking the following practice examination. First, let's look at some common-sense tips for test-taking:

✦ **Don't leave any questions unanswered.** Since there is no penalty for guessing, be sure to answer all questions — even if you are only making a guess.

✦ **Use the process of elimination** in multiple-choice questions. Even if you do not know the right answer, it may be clear that certain choices are wrong. Choices will be wrong if they relate to a different time or place, have no connection with the question, or are simply inaccurate statements. After eliminating the wrong choices, choose the best answer of those that remain.

✦ **Underline any key words** in the question that you think are central to what it asks. If an unfamiliar word is used, try breaking it down into other words that are familiar to you. See if looking at the prefix *(start of the word)*, root, or suffix *(word ending)* helps you to understand the meaning of the word.

Taking this test will help you identify areas that you may still need to study. Good luck!

GLOBAL HISTORY PRACTICE EXAMINATION

This practice test has three parts:

Part I has 50 multiple-choice questions;

Part II has one thematic essay; and

Part III has one document-based essay.

PART 1: MULTIPLE-CHOICE QUESTIONS

1   The herding of animals and the growing of crops were advances made during the
    1 Commercial Revolution   3 Paleolithic Age
    2 Shang Dynasty   4 Neolithic Revolution

2   Which of the following is a primary source about ancient Egypt?
    1 a college textbook on ancient Egypt
    2 an Internet site about the pyramids
    3 a magazine article about life in ancient Egypt
    4 hieroglyphic writing on an ancient Egyptian temple wall

3   Buildings such as the pyramids in Egypt, the Parthenon in Greece, and the Colosseum
    in Rome reflect each society's
    1 strategic location   3 belief in democracy
    2 cultural values   4 military power

4   The Ten Commandments and the Five Pillars of Faith are similar in that both
    1 establish a classless society   3 provide guidelines for moral conduct
    2 consist of prayers for salvation 4 promise a happy and easy life

5   Which condition led to the development of the Renaissance period?
    1 rigid social classes   3 questioning of authority
    2 religious uniformity   4 mass education

6   Which achievement was an important contribution of Muslim culture to world civili-
    zation?
    1 the development of perspective and realism in painting
    2 new advances in science and math
    3 the invention of gunpowder, silk, and porcelain
    4 the separation of church and state

7   The Mandate of Heaven in Zhou China was most similar to the
    1 divine right of kings in Western Europe
    2 concept of liberty in the French Revolution
    3 dictatorship of the proletariat under Communism
    4 the Nazi doctrine of racial superiority

8 Which quotation best reflects Confucian beliefs in ancient China?
   1 "An eye for an eye and a tooth for a tooth."
   2 "One of a person's greatest social obligations is loyalty to family."
   3 "The way of nature is to work through opposites."
   4 "The end justifies the means."

Base your answer to question 9 on this map and your knowledge of global history.

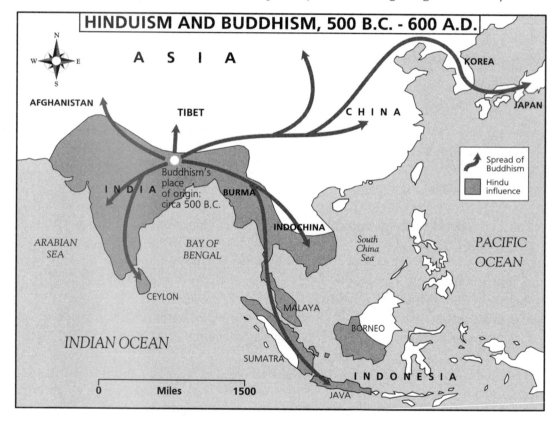

HINDUISM AND BUDDHISM, 500 B.C. - 600 A.D.

9 Which concept is best illustrated by the information on the map?
   1 spread of democracy   3 cultural diffusion
   2 Pax Romana   4 caste system

10 Which statement best describes a result of the Crusades?
   1 Europeans established lasting control over most of the Middle East.
   2 Muslim warriors conquered Spain.
   3 Europeans became more tolerant of non-Christian religions.
   4 Europeans were exposed to new ideas.

11 A lasting effect of the Byzantine Empire was the
 1 development of Islam   3 emergence of Buddhism
 2 spread of Orthodox Christianity   4 decline of Zoroastrianism

12 Which characteristic was shared by both Japanese and European feudalism?
 1 Land was exchanged for military service and obligations.
 2 Government was provided by a central bureaucracy of civil servants.
 3 Candidates took written examinations to serve in the emperor's government.
 4 Religious officials ran the government.

13 Four key events in global history are listed below.

> A. The fall of the Roman empire
> B. The overthrow of the Qing (Manchu) dynasty
> C. The construction of the Great Wall of China
> D. The fall of Constantinople

What is the correct chronological order for these events?
 1 B → A → C → D   3 C → A → D → B
 2 A → D → C → B   4 D → B → C → A

14 Which chapter heading is correctly paired with a person associated with the event?
 1 "Mali Ruler Visits Egypt" - Michelangelo
 2 "Artist Paints Sistine Chapel Ceiling" - Martin Luther
 3 "Mongols Invade Northern China" - Chinggis Khan
 4 "Clergyman Questions Roman Catholic Church" - Mansa Musa

15 The success of the West African kingdoms of Ghana, Mali, and Songhai rested on
 1 their control of the salt and gold trade
 2 the massive fortifications of their cities
 3 their use of gunpowder and cannons
 4 their domination of the Transatlantic slave trade

16 One way in which the Seljuk Turks and Mongols were similar is that they both
 1 emerged from Central Asia
 2 were defeated by the Byzantine Empire
 3 traded along the Silk Road with Rome
 4 developed unique forms of Christianity

Base your answer to question 17 on the picture on the right and your knowledge of global history.

17 This painting represents an artistic style of which culture?
   1 T'ang China   3 Renaissance Italy
   2 Roman Empire   4 Kingdom of Songhai

---

18 Isaac Newton promoted the conviction that scientific knowledge is based on
   1 the wisdom of past civilizations
   2 emotions and feelings
   3 observation, experimentation, and mathematics
   4 the teachings of the Catholic Church

19 A laissez-faire capitalist would most likely advocate
   1 a mercantilist colonial policy
   2 the non-involvement of government in relations with workers
   3 the regulation of big business by government
   4 a classless society

20 A study of the Maya, Aztec, and Inca cultures shows that these Native American peoples
   1 produced rich and complex civilizations
   2 had extensive contacts with ancient Greece and Rome
   3 spoke similar languages
   4 were peaceful before contact with Europeans

21 A lasting impact of the European encounter with the pre-Columbian civilizations of the Americas was
   1 the introduction of new foods to Africa, Asia, and Europe
   2 the end of slavery in Africa
   3 the spread of gunpowder to Europe and Africa
   4 the birth of the world's first democracies

22 A major characteristic of the Commercial Revolution in Western Europe was
   1 the rise of capitalism
   2 the development of local handicrafts
   3 greater respect for the rights of indigenous people
   4 the emergence of the manorial system

23 Both the encomienda system in Spanish America and the manorial system in medieval
Europe were based on
   1 a prosperous middle class   3 strong central government
   2 forced peasant labor   4 a capitalist economy

24 Which statement is best supported by a study of the Transatlantic slave trade?
   1 It discouraged warfare among African tribes.
   2 It destroyed much of Africa's rich cultural heritage.
   3 African slavery in the "New World" was limited to the English colonies.
   4 Spanish leaders in South America strongly opposed importing slaves.

25 Which two individuals created large empires in Asia?
   1 Akbar the Great and Chinggis Khan   3 Hernando Cortés and Shah Jahan
   2 Mansa Musa and Peter the Great   4 Charlemagne and Montezuma

26 A major policy of the Tokugawa Shogunate was the
   1 destruction of the samurai class   3 banning of foreigners from Japan
   2 restoration of full power to the emperor 4 opening of Japan to Western influence

Base your answer to question 27 on this table and your knowledge of global studies.

THE WORLD'S LARGEST URBAN AREAS BY POPULATION
(in thousands)

1350 B.C.		1600 A.D.	
Thebes, Egypt	100	Beijing, China	706
Memphis, Egypt	74	Istanbul, Turkey	700
Babylon, Iraq	54	Agra, India	500
Chengchow, China	40	Cairo, Egypt	400
Hattushash, Turkey	40	Osaka, Japan	400

27 In both 1350 B.C. and 1600 A.D., most large urban centers were located in
   1 Eastern and Western Europe   3 North and Central America
   2 East Asia and the Middle East   4 Africa and South America

28 What would most likely be included in a description of an area's physical geography?
   1 customs and traditions   3 systems of government
   2 landforms and bodies of water   4 distribution of goods and services

29 In an outline, one of these is a main topic, and the others are sub-topics. Which is the *main topic*?

    1 Storming of the Bastille   3 Declaration of the Rights of Man
    2 Reign of Terror   4 French Revolution

30 Alexander the Great and Chinggis Khan both had the common goal of
    1 resisting the introduction of new technology
    2 establishing governments based on democratic principles
    3 freeing their nations from foreign domination
    4 expanding the size of their empires

31 A primary goal of the statesmen at the Congress of Vienna was to
    1 satisfy nationalist aspirations in Italy, Poland, Greece, and Belgium
    2 establish a balance of power among leading European states
    3 promote democratic governments in Europe
    4 create a League of Nations to keep peace in Europe

32 In Western Europe, which development was a cause of the other three?
    1 increased urban population   3 rise of the factory system
    2 increased air and water pollution   4 cheaper textiles

33 Which statement about nationalism is most accurate?
    1 Nationalism may promote or hinder the unity of particular states.
    2 Nationalism is always based on a common language.
    3 Nationalism prevents the rise of militarism.
    4 Nationalism promotes rule by monarchs.

34 Giuseppe Garibaldi and Simon Bolivar were similar in that both
    1 encouraged a spirit of nationalism among their people
    2 denied voting rights to citizens after gaining control of their nations
    3 opposed the territorial expansion of their nations
    4 followed the ideas of Marx in establishing systems of government

35 European imperialism in the 19th century was generally motivated by
    1 a desire to spread democracy
    2 the desire for expanded economic opportunities
    3 an admiration for the cultures of other regions
    4 a desire to protect the political rights of native peoples

Base your answer to question 36 on this graph and your knowledge of global history.

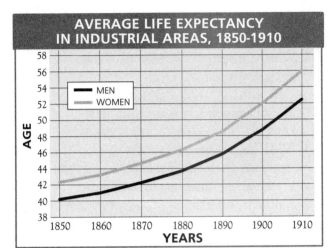

AVERAGE LIFE EXPECTANCY IN INDUSTRIAL AREAS, 1850-1910

36 According to the graph, which statement is most accurate?
1 On average, men lived longer than women.
2 The period 1850 to 1910 saw the spread of European imperialism.
3 Medical care declined during the Industrial Revolution.
4 Life expectancy in industrial areas gradually increased from 1850 to 1910.

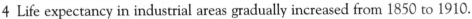

37 The Sepoy Mutiny (1857) and the Boxer Rebellion (1899) were reactions to
1 rapid industrialization   3 Mongol rule
2 European imperialism   4 World War I

38 Kemal Atatürk, Sun Yat-Sen, and Kwame Nkrumah are most closely associated with
1 commanding armies in major wars 3 economic reform
2 leading nationalist movements   4 cultural achievements

39 Which was a direct result of the Russian Revolution of 1917?
1 Russia became the world's first Communist nation.
2 Trade between Russia and the United States increased.
3 Christianity was adopted as the official state religion of Russia.
4 Russia entered World War I on the side of the Allies.

40 In the 1930s and 1940s, Fascist regimes in Germany and Italy emphasized
1 empathy toward African nations
2 protection of human rights
3 war as an instrument of foreign policy
4 support of free expression

41 The steppes of Central Asia are most similar in topography to the
1 mountains of Switzerland   3 rain forests of South America
2 deserts of the Middle East   4 savannas of Africa

Base your answer to question 42 on the cartoon and your knowledge of global history.

42 Which foreign policy concept is shown in the cartoon?
1 détente   3 perestroika
2 appeasement   4 containment

43 Which action best illustrates the foreign policy of containment?
1 settlement of an international dispute by arbitration
2 sending U.S. troops to South Korea to oppose the North Korean invasion
3 suspension of U.S. financial support for the United Nations if it takes actions that are contrary to U.S. national goals
4 the U.S. failure to resist the Communist takeover of China in 1949

44 A key problem that faced the Austro-Hungarian Empire, the Ottoman Empire, and the Soviet Union was the
1 migration of people to the cities   3 inability to produce new weapons
2 monopoly of the traditional church   4 tension among ethnic groups

45 Which generalization is best supported by such developments as Japanese investment in Southeast Asia and the reliance of many Western European nations on oil from the Middle East?
1 Most nations are now adopting socialist economies.
2 Nations that control vital resources no longer influence world markets.
3 The goal of most economic planners is to increase national self-sufficiency.
4 The nations of the world have become economically interdependent.

46 The rise of independent nations in Asia and Africa after World War II illustrates the
1 spread of the Cold War to the Third World
2 resolution of ethnic conflicts in these regions
3 decline of European political dominance
4 failure of nationalist movements

47 The Suez Canal, the Panama Canal, and the Dardanelles Straits are similar in that they
1 are strategic waterways on major trade routes   3 are man-made waterways
2 were once part of the Mongol Empire   4 were built by the Roman Empire

48 The experiences of France in Vietnam and the Soviet Union in Afghanistan suggest
  1 that Communism is a growing force in the world
  2 that guerrilla forces can never win wars without aid from other nations
  3 that large scale industry is necessary to win wars
  4 that powerful nations cannot always enforce their will on others

49 Which region is important because of its strategic location, major oil reserves, and historical significance as the birthplace of three major religions?
  1 Latin America   3 Western Europe
  2 Southeast Asia   4 Middle East

Base your answer to question 50 on this table and on your knowledge of global history.

ESTIMATED WORLD POPULATION, 1650-1850 *(in millions)*

CONTINENT	1650	1750	1850
Africa	100	95	95
Asia	327	475	741
South America	12	11	33
North America	1	1	26
Europe (including Russia)	103	144	274
Australia	2	2	2

50 Which factor most likely explains the absence of growth in Africa's population during these two centuries?
  1 crop failures caused by poor climatic conditions
  2 voluntary emigration of Africans to Europe and Asia
  3 forced migration of enslaved Africans to the Americas
  4 diseases introduced to Africa from the Americas

PART II: THEMATIC ESSAY QUESTION

Directions: Write a well-organized essay that includes an introduction, several paragraphs explaining your position, and a conclusion.

Theme: Political Systems

> Revolutions often seek to reform political, economic, and social conditions yet lead to repression.

continued...

Task:

> Choose **two** revolutions from your study of global history and geography.
>
> For *each* revolution:
> * Describe the revolution.
> * Show *how*, in seeking political, economic and social reform, it led to repression.

You may use any example from your study of global history and geography. Some suggestions you may wish to consider include: English Revolution (1640), French Revolution (1789), Russian Revolution (1917), Chinese Revolution (1949), Cuban Revolution (1959), and Islamic Fundamentalist Revolution in Iran (1979).

You are not limited to these suggestions.

PART III: DOCUMENT-BASED ESSAY QUESTION

> **This task is based on the accompanying documents (1-7). Some of these documents have been edited for the purposes of this task. This task is designed to test your ability to work with historical documents. As you analyze the documents, take into account both the source of each document and the author's point of view.**
>
> *Directions:* Read the documents in Part A and answer the questions after each document. Then read the directions for Part B and write your essay.
>
> **Historical Context:**
> Throughout history, the introduction of new technologies has often been accompanied by significant social, economic, and political change.
>
> **Task:**
> Discuss the impact that technological change has had on history.

Part A — Short Answer

Directions: Analyze the documents and answer the questions that follow each document.

Document 1:

> "When food production became more efficient, there was time to develop the arts and sciences. Agriculture probably required a far greater discipline than did any form of food collecting. Seeds had to be planted at certain seasons, some protection had to be given to growing plants, harvests had to be reaped, stored and divided. It has been suggested that writing may have come into existence because records were needed by agricultural administrators."
>
> — Charles Heiser, *Seed to Civilization*, 1981

1. How did technological changes in agriculture bring about other changes? _____

Document 2:

> "The most significant invention in the history of warfare prior to gunpowder was the stirrup. In conjunction with a saddle, stirrups welded horse and rider into a single organism. The long lance could now be held at rest under the right armpit. The increase in violence was immense."
> — Lynn White, Jr.
> *The Expansion of Technology, 500-1500*

2. How did the invention of the stirrup for mounted knights transform warfare in the Middle Ages?

Document 3:

3. How did the Industrial Revolution affect the production of cotton cloth in Britain?

_____

_____

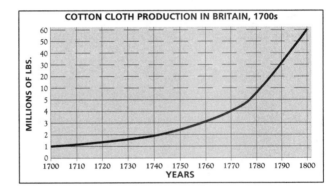

COTTON CLOTH PRODUCTION IN BRITAIN, 1700s

MILLIONS OF LBS.

60 50 40 30 20 10 5 4 3 2 1 0

1700 1710 1720 1730 1740 1750 1760 1770 1780 1790 1800
YEARS

Document 4:

> "Labour in an industrial society ... is overwhelmingly the labour of 'proletarians' who have no source of income except a cash wage ... mechanized labour imposes a regularity, routine and monotony quite unlike pre-industrial work ... labour in the industrial age took place in the unprecedented environment of the big city ... And what cities! It was not merely that smoke hung over them and filth impregnated them, that elementary public services — water supply, sanitation, street-cleaning — could not keep pace with the mass migration ... But more than this: the city destroyed society."
> — Eric Hobsbawm, *Industry and Empire*, 1969

4. What is Hobsbawm's view of the effect of the Industrial Revolution on workers?

Document 5:

This photo shows the ruins of a Shinto shrine in Nagasaki, Japan, after an atomic bomb had been dropped on the city in August, 1945.

5. What does this picture show about the impact of atomic weapons?

_____

Document 6:

> "The speed with which computers have spread is ... well known. Costs have dropped so sharply and capacity has risen so spectacularly that, according to one authority, 'If the auto industry had done what the computer industry has done in the last 30 years, a Rolls-Royce would cost $2.50 and would get 2,000,000 miles to the gallon.'"
>
> —Alvin Toffler, *The Third Wave*

6. What does Toffler see as one important achievement of the computer industry?

Document 7:

7. What two nations produce almost one-third of the world's pollution?

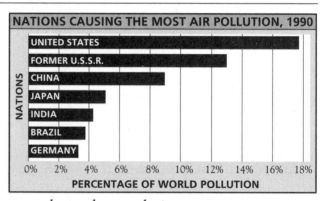

NATIONS CAUSING THE MOST AIR POLLUTION, 1990

NATIONS: UNITED STATES, FORMER U.S.S.R., CHINA, JAPAN, INDIA, BRAZIL, GERMANY

PERCENTAGE OF WORLD POLLUTION

_____

Part B — Essay

Directions:

• Write a well-organized essay that includes an introduction, several paragraphs, and a conclusion.
• Use evidence from the documents to support your response.
• Do not simply repeat the contents of the documents.
• Include specific related information.

Task: Using information from the documents and your knowledge of global history and geography, write an essay in which you:

Discuss the impact that technological change has had on history.